slow cooker

slow cooker

From tasty stews to comforting casseroles

This edition published in 2011

LOVE FOOD is an imprint of Parragon Books Ltd

Parragon
Queen Street House
4 Queen Street
Bath BA1 1HE, UK

ISBN 978-1-4454-4008-8

Printed in China

Notes for the reader
This book uses both metric and imperial measurements. Follow the same units of measurement throughout; do not mix metric and imperial. All spoon measurements are level: teaspoons are assumed to be 5 ml, and tablespoons are assumed to be 15 ml. Unless otherwise stated, milk is assumed to be full fat, eggs and individual vegetables are medium, and pepper is freshly ground black pepper.

The times given are an approximate guide only. Preparation times differ according to the techniques used by different people and cooking times may also vary from those given. Optional ingredients, variations or serving suggestions have not been included in the calculations.

Recipes using raw or very lightly cooked eggs should be avoided by infants, the elderly, pregnant women, convalescents and anyone suffering from an illness. Pregnant and breastfeeding women are advised to avoid eating peanuts and peanut products. Sufferers from nut allergies should be aware that some of the ready-made ingredients used in the recipes in this book may contain nuts. Always check the packaging before use.

Contents

Life seems to grow more hectic by the day and there never seems to be enough time to do all the things we have to, let alone those we want to. We struggle to balance work and family commitments and now we are all being told to take more exercise and eat a healthier diet.

Introduction

The solution to the second part of this problem is the slow cooker. The idea is very simple – you put the ingredients in the cooker, switch it on (it's electric), then safely go to work, go shopping, take the kids to the football, do whatever you want to do and some hours later, come home and you have a delicious meal waiting for you. The slow cooker cooks the food at a temperature high enough to ensure that microbes are destroyed and the ingredients become tender, but low enough to prevent liquid from evaporating and the food burning. This also means that if your meeting overruns or you're caught in traffic, your meal will not be spoiled. It will be ready when you are ready to eat it.

The hardware

The slow cooker consists of a base unit, which contains the heating element, and an inner ceramic cooking pot. In modern cookers, this pot is invariably removable but in some older models it is fixed. It is supplied with a lid, usually made of heatproof glass nowadays. This lets you check on progress without lifting it and so lowering the temperature inside the pot. The base unit may be encased in a heatproof material and its handles and the handle on the lid are very likely to be cool-touch. Note, however, that the inner pot will become very hot during cooking and you should always wear oven gloves when handling it. The base unit stands securely on two or more feet.

The cooker is usually controlled by a dial, although older models may simply have a switch. Typical dial positions are 'off', 'low', 'high' and 'auto'. Some cookers also include 'medium'. The older switch controls are 'low' and 'high' but do not always include 'off'. Such cookers must, therefore, be switched off at the electrical socket.

The precise design of individual cookers varies and it is important that you read the manufacturer's instructions. These will give guidelines about using, cleaning and storing your particular model.

A variety of sizes is available to suit your individual needs, but remember that the base unit can mislead you into thinking that the cooking pot holds more than it really does. A 3.5-litre/6-pint working capacity is suitable for most families and is not so large that it is difficult to find storage space. Round and oval cookers are produced and both have benefits and drawbacks.

What you can cook

The slow cooker is surprisingly versatile, although it cannot be used for every kind of cooking. There must be liquid of some sort in the cooker for it to function properly, so it is ideal for casseroles, stews, soups and pasta sauces. You can also use it as a water bath for delicate foods, such as egg custards, which will work only if cooked slowly at a low temperature. It is invaluable for serving hot punch or mulled wine at a party, too. While it is perfect for pot roasts, it cannot be used for traditional roasts or, indeed, anything that is normally cooked at a high temperature in the oven, a frying pan or a deep-fryer, or under the grill. Nor is it suitable for foods, such as pasta, that require vigorous boiling, as the temperature always remains below 100°C/212°F.

The slow cooker works as well for chicken casseroles as it does for vegetables curries and there are few ingredients that cannot be cooked this way. It is especially good for less tender cuts of meat, such as stewing steak, and, as these are usually less expensive, it's good for the family budget as well. Long cooking at a low temperature tenderizes the meat while at the same time condensation on the inside of the lid forms a seal that keeps the meat succulent.

Vegetarian dishes and vegetable accompaniments also work well. However some, especially root vegetables, take a very long time to cook. For those used to the convention of cooking vegetables briefly in the minimum amount of liquid, it can come as something of a shock when they first start using a slow cooker to look at the timing and amount of liquid. Be assured, however, that texture, colour, flavour and nutritional content will all be retained. On the other hand, cooking lentils and dried beans is simplicity itself – and there is no need to worry about the liquid boiling over or boiling dry.

You can use the slow cooker for fish and seafood, but the technique is slightly different as they cannot withstand prolonged cooking and will lose their flavour and disintegrate. Use the slow cooker in the usual way for preparing the base of a stew or sauce with, for example, onion, tomatoes and other vegetables, then add the fish or seafood for the last part of the cooking time. They always need to be cooked on the high setting and take 30–60 minutes.

Using the slow cooker

No special preparation is required for meat, poultry and vegetables and these may be sliced, diced or chopped in the usual way. It is worth trimming off visible fat from any meat and, of course, this is healthier too. (You can also skim off any fat from the surface when the dish has finished cooking.) When preparing root vegetables, you may find it helpful to slice more thinly or chop more finely than you are used to when cooking on the hob or in the oven.

You can put all the ingredients straight into the slow cooker, add the liquid and switch on. However, meat and poultry look more attractive and retain more flavour if they are lightly browned first. Some recipes in this book recommend tossing them in flour before browning. Similarly, onions and some other vegetables benefit from being lightly softened in a frying pan with oil or melted butter for about 5 minutes before adding them to the cooker.

Mainly common-sense kitchen rules apply. Most dried pulses still need to be soaked before cooking and those that should be pre-boiled vigorously for 15 minutes – aduki, black, borlotti, red kidney and black-eyed beans – should still be treated this way. After pre-boiling, drain them well before adding to the slow cooker.

There are a few watch points when using a slow cooker. Frozen foods should always be thawed thoroughly before they are added. It has always been necessary to thaw meat and poultry before cooking, whatever the method, to safeguard health. With the slow cooker, even vegetables such as frozen peas must be thawed first. Otherwise they will dramatically lower the temperature of the cooker and the optimum temperature may not be regained, resulting in uncooked food and increased risk to health. It is also a good idea to remove ingredients that have been marinating in the refrigerator about 30 minutes before adding them to the slow cooker to let them return to room temperature. For a similar reason, it is usually advisable to bring the liquid to be added-stock, water, fruit juice, etc.-to boiling point before it is added to the cooker. This ensures that the optimum temperature is reached as quickly as possible. As a general rule, you will need slightly less liquid than required in recipes for conventional cooking because less will evaporate. Finally, it is best not to add dairy products, such as cream and yogurt, until the last 30 minutes of the cooking time to prevent them from curdling.

When you are ready to cook, place the slow cooker on a level work surface and make sure that the cord does not hang over the edge. Check that the dial is on the 'off' position before you plug the cooker into the socket. Remove the cooking pot from the base unit to avoid spilling ingredients and splashing liquid into the base when you are adding them. (This is not a concern with older models as the cooking pot is sealed to the base unit.)

Place the prepared ingredients in the cooking pot, but do not fill it more than about two-thirds full to allow room for expansion and for the heat to spread easily and evenly. Return the pot to the base unit, place the lid on top, and switch the cooker on. Cook on the setting specified in the recipe for the time suggested. Do not remove the lid during cooking, however tempting it is to prod around with a wooden spoon, because this will lower the temperature and it takes quite a long time for the cooker to return to the optimum. Stirring part of the way through the cooking time is recommended in very few recipes, and in some others, delicate ingredients, such as mushrooms and prawns, are added towards the end of the cooking time. Try not to lift the lid during the first half of the cooking time, then stir or add at the appropriate time and re-cover with the lid as soon as possible.

The cooking times in the recipes are guidelines and not precise. Many different things can cause a variation, from the thickness of vegetable slices to the freshness of dried legumes. As it's almost impossible to overcook a dish in the slow cooker, with the exception of fish and seafood, this should not be a problem. As you get used to using it, you will acquire a 'feel' for cooking times. Recipes state whether the setting should be high or low – the former cooks twice as quickly as the latter. As a general guide, soups, stews and sauces are best cooked on low, while legumes, fish and some vegetable dishes are best cooked on high. Manufacturers recommend that you do not leave the cooker completely unattended on the high setting as there is a slight risk of the liquid drying out. If you have to go out or you want to cook overnight, use the auto setting if you have one because the cooker starts cooking on the high setting and then switches to low.

Safety tips
• Make sure that the cooker is out of the reach of children and that the cord does not hang over the edge of the work surface.
• Do not switch on the slow cooker without the cooking pot in position.
• Do not use the slow cooker if the cable, plug, base unit, cooking pot or lid is damaged.
• Never put ingredients directly into the base of the slow cooker.
• Do not reheat food in the slow cooker.
• Make sure that food is cooked through before serving. This is especially important with meat products, pork and poultry. Pierce the thickest part with the point of a sharp knife and if the juices show any traces of pink or red, continue to cook for a little longer. When the juices run clear, the meat is cooked through.
• Don't peer into the slow cooker when you first lift the lid as the steam that billows out might scald your face.
• Always use oven gloves when lifting out the cooking pot.

guide to recipe key

IOI	SERVES 4	Guide to serving portions
	10 MINUTES	Preparation time
	10 MINUTES	Cooking time

To Start

A great first course, this colourful country soup also makes a delicious light lunch served with Greek poppy seed bread.

Greek Bean & Vegetable Soup

Ingredients

500g/1 lb 2 oz dried haricot beans,
  soaked in cold water overnight

2 onions, finely chopped

2 garlic cloves, finely chopped

2 potatoes, chopped

2 carrots, chopped

2 tomatoes, peeled and chopped

2 celery sticks, chopped

4 tbsp extra-virgin olive oil

1 bay leaf

salt and pepper

To garnish

12 black olives, stoned
  and halved

2 tbsp chopped fresh chives

Serves 4–6

Preparation time: 15 minutes,
plus overnight soaking

Cooking time: 12 hours

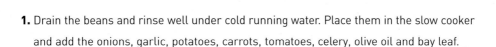

1. Drain the beans and rinse well under cold running water. Place them in the slow cooker and add the onions, garlic, potatoes, carrots, tomatoes, celery, olive oil and bay leaf.

2. Pour in 2 litres/3½ pints boiling water, making sure that all the ingredients are fully submerged. Cover and cook on low for 12 hours until the beans are tender.

3. Remove and discard the bay leaf. Season the soup to taste with salt and pepper and stir in the olives and chives. Ladle into warmed soup bowls or large mugs and serve.

This is a two-for-the-price-of-one dish as you can serve the broth as a first course and serve the chicken for the main course.

Cock-a-Leekie Soup

Ingredients

12 prunes, stoned, or 12 ready-to-eat prunes

4 chicken portions

450 g/1 lb leeks, sliced

1.4 litres/2½ pints hot chicken or beef stock

1 bouquet garni

salt and pepper

 Serves 6–8

 Preparation time: 15 minutes, plus 7 hours soaking

 Cooking time: 7½ hours

1. If using ordinary prunes, place them in a bowl and add cold water to cover. Set aside to soak while the soup is cooking.

2. Place the chicken portions and leeks in the slow cooker. Pour in the stock and add the bouquet garni. Cover and cook on low for 7 hours.

3. If you are going to serve the chicken with the soup, remove it from the cooker with a slotted spoon and cut the meat off the bones. Cut it into bite-sized pieces and return it to the cooker. Otherwise, leave the chicken portions in the slow cooker.

4. Drain the prunes, if necessary. Add the prunes to the soup and season to taste with salt and pepper. Re-cover and cook on high for 30 minutes.

5. Remove and discard the bouquet garni. Either ladle the soup, including the cut-up chicken, into warm bowls or remove the chicken portions and keep warm for the main course, then ladle the broth into warmed bowls. Serve immediately.

Bacon & Lentil Soup

Ingredients

450 g/1 lb thick, rindless smoked bacon
　rashers, diced

1 onion, chopped

2 carrots, sliced

2 celery sticks, chopped

1 turnip, chopped

1 large potato, chopped

85 g/3 oz green lentils

1 bouquet garni

1 litre/1¾ pints chicken stock or water

salt and pepper

 Serves 4

 Preparation time: 15 minutes,
plus 12–15 minutes pre-cooking

Cooking time: 8–9 hours

---

1. Heat a large, heavy-based saucepan. Add the bacon and cook over a low heat, stirring frequently, for 4–5 minutes, until the fat runs. Add the onion, carrots, celery, turnip and potato and cook, stirring frequently, for 5 minutes.

2. Add the lentils and bouquet garni and pour in the stock. Bring to the boil, then transfer the mixture to the slow cooker. Cover and cook on low for 8–9 hours, or until the lentils are tender.

3. Remove and discard the bouquet garni and season the soup to taste with salt and pepper, if necessary. Ladle into warmed soup bowls and serve.

Not only is this spicy warm dip a tasty starter, but it is also an ideal party snack. Serve it with a selection of dippers if you like.

Tex-Mex Bean Dip

Ingredients

2 tbsp sunflower oil

1 onion, finely chopped

2 garlic cloves, finely chopped

2–3 fresh green chillies, deseeded and finely chopped

400 g/14 oz canned refried beans or red kidney beans

2 tbsp chilli sauce or taco sauce

6 tbsp hot vegetable stock

115 g/4 oz Cheddar cheese, grated

salt and pepper

1 fresh red chilli, deseeded and shredded, to garnish

tortilla chips, to serve

 Serves 4

 Preparation time: 15 minutes, plus 5 minutes pre-cooking

 Cooking time: 2 hours

---

1. Heat the oil in a large, heavy-based frying pan. Add the onion, garlic and chillies and cook, stirring occasionally, over a low heat for 5 minutes until the onion is soft and translucent. Transfer to the slow cooker.

2. Add the refried beans to the slow cooker. If using red kidney beans, drain well and rinse under cold running water. Reserve 2 tablespoons of the beans and mash the remainder coarsely with a potato masher. Add all the beans to the slow cooker.

3. Add the sauce, stock and cheese, season with salt and pepper and stir well. Cover and cook on low for 2 hours.

4. Transfer the dip to a serving bowl, garnish with shredded red chilli and serve warm with tortilla chips on the side.

An attractive vegetarian starter, this lightly spiced dish can also be served as an accompaniment to chicken or simply grilled fish.

Louisiana Courgettes

Ingredients

1 kg/2 lb 4 oz courgettes, thickly sliced

1 onion, finely chopped

2 garlic cloves, finely chopped

2 red peppers, deseeded and chopped

5 tbsp hot vegetable stock

4 tomatoes, peeled and chopped

25 g/1 oz butter, diced

salt and cayenne pepper

Serves 6

Preparation time: 15 minutes

Cooking time: 2½ hours

1. Place the courgettes, onion, garlic and red peppers in the slow cooker and season to taste with salt and cayenne pepper. Pour in the stock and mix well.

2. Sprinkle the chopped tomatoes on top and dot with the butter. Cover and cook on high for 2½ hours until tender.

Messy but delicious, chicken wings are also good to serve as party nibbles – just increase the quantity.

Sweet-and-Sour Chicken Wings

Ingredients
1 kg/2 lb 4 oz chicken wings, tips removed
2 celery sticks, chopped
700 ml/1¼ pints hot chicken stock
2 tbsp cornflour
3 tbsp white wine vinegar or rice vinegar
3 tbsp dark soy sauce
5 tbsp sweet chilli sauce
55 g/2 oz brown sugar
400 g/14 oz canned pineapple
   chunks in juice, drained

200 g/7 oz canned sliced bamboo
   shoots, drained and rinsed
½ green pepper, deseeded and thinly
   sliced
½ red pepper, deseeded and thinly sliced
salt

🍽 Serves 4–6

🥄 Preparation time: 10 minutes,
   plus 10 minutes for the sauce

🧤 Cooking time: 5 hours

1. Put the chicken wings and celery in the slow cooker and season with salt. Pour in the chicken stock, cover and cook on low for 5 hours.

2. Drain the chicken wings, reserving 350 ml/12 fl oz of the stock, and keep warm. Pour the reserved stock into a saucepan and stir in the cornflour. Add the vinegar, soy sauce and chilli sauce. Place over a medium heat and stir in the sugar. Cook, stirring constantly, for 5 minutes, or until the sugar has dissolved completely and the sauce is thickened, smooth and clear.

3. Lower the heat, stir in the pineapple, bamboo shoots and peppers and simmer gently for 2–3 minutes. Stir in the chicken wings until they are thoroughly coated, then transfer to serving bowls.

Chickpeas have a deliciously nutty flavour that works well with a herb dressing. They are notorious for taking ages to cook, so the slow cooker solves the problem.

Warm Chickpea Salad

Ingredients

225 g/8 oz dried chickpeas, soaked
  overnight in cold water and drained
115 g/4 oz stoned black olives
4 spring onions, finely chopped
fresh parsley sprigs, to garnish
crusty bread, to serve

For the dressing

2 tbsp red wine vinegar
2 tbsp mixed chopped fresh herbs, such
  as parsley, rosemary and thyme
3 garlic cloves, very finely chopped
125 ml/4 fl oz extra-virgin olive oil
salt and pepper

 Serves 6

 Preparation time: 10 minutes,
plus overnight soaking

 Cooking time: 12 hours

1. Place the chickpeas in the slow cooker and add sufficient boiling water to cover. Cover and cook on low for 12 hours.

2. Drain well and transfer to a bowl. Stir in the olives and spring onions.

3. To make the dressing, whisk together the vinegar, herbs and garlic in a jug and season with salt and pepper to taste. Gradually whisk in the olive oil. Pour the dressing over the still-warm chickpeas and toss lightly to coat. Garnish with the parsley sprigs and serve warm with crusty bread.

Served with a quick and easy sauce and a salad, these attractive moulds make an unusual vegetarian main course.

Aubergine Timbales

Ingredients
2 aubergines
3 tbsp olive oil, plus extra for greasing
2 onions, finely chopped
2 red peppers, deseeded and chopped
1 large tomato, peeled and chopped
6 tbsp milk
2 egg yolks
pinch of ground cinnamon
85 g/3 oz crispbread, finely crushed
salt and pepper
fresh coriander sprigs, to garnish

For the sauce
300 ml/10 fl oz soured cream
3–4 tbsp sun-dried tomato purée
(optional)

 Serves 4

Preparation time: 15 minutes, plus 20–25 minutes pre-cooking

Cooking time: 2 hours

---

1. Halve the aubergines and scoop out the flesh with a spoon. Reserve the shells and dice the flesh. Heat the oil in a large, heavy-based frying pan. Add the onions and cook over a low heat, stirring occasionally, for 5 minutes. Add the diced aubergines, red peppers and tomato and cook, stirring occasionally, for 15–20 minutes, until all the vegetables are soft. Remove the pan from the heat.

2. Transfer the mixture to a food processor or blender and process to a purée, then scrape into a bowl. Beat together the milk, egg yolks, cinnamon and salt and pepper in a jug, then stir into the vegetable purée.

3. Brush 4 ramekins or cups with oil and sprinkle with the crispbread crumbs to coat. Tip out any excess. Mix about three-quarters of the remaining crumbs into the vegetable purée. Slice the aubergine shells into strips and use them to line the ramekins, leaving the ends protruding above the rims. Spoon the filling into the ramekins, sprinkle with the remaining crumbs and fold the overlapping ends over.

4. Cover with foil and place in the slow cooker. Pour in sufficient boiling water to come about one-third of the way up the sides of the ramekins. Cover and cook on high for 2 hours.

5. To make the sauce, lightly beat the soured cream and add the tomato purée to taste, if desired. Season with salt and pepper. Lift the ramekins out of the cooker and remove the foil. Invert onto serving plates and serve with the sauce, garnished with coriander sprigs.

This traditional American dish can be served on its own with plenty of warm, fresh bread or as an accompaniment to roast pork.

Boston Baked Beans

Ingredients

450 g/1 lb dried white haricot beans, soaked overnight in cold water and drained

115 g/4 oz salt pork, soaked in cold water for 3 hours and drained

3 tbsp molasses or black treacle

3 tbsp muscovado sugar

2 tsp dry mustard

1 onion, chopped

salt and pepper

 Serves 4–6

 Preparation time: 15 minutes, plus overnight soaking

 Cooking time: 3 + 11 hours (14 hours in total)

1. Place the beans in the slow cooker and add about 1.4 litres/2½ pints boiling water so that they are covered. Cover and cook on high for 3 hours. Meanwhile, cut the salt pork into chunks.

2. Drain the beans, reserving 225 ml/8 fl oz of the cooking liquid. Mix the reserved liquid with the molasses, sugar, mustard and 1 teaspoon of salt.

3. Return the beans to the slow cooker and add the salt pork, onion and the molasses mixture. Stir, then cover and cook on low for 11 hours.

4. Adjust the seasoning and serve immediately.

These tasty stuffed cabbage rolls make a great vegetarian starter but can also be served as a main course.

Cabbage Roulades with Tomato Sauce

Ingredients

225 g/8 oz mixed nuts, finely ground
2 onions, finely chopped
1 garlic clove, finely chopped
2 celery sticks, finely chopped
115 g/4 oz Cheddar cheese, grated
1 tsp thyme, finely chopped
2 eggs
1 tsp yeast extract
12 large green cabbage leaves

Tomato sauce

2 tbsp sunflower oil
2 onions, chopped

2 garlic cloves, finely chopped
600 g/1 lb 5 oz canned
   chopped tomatoes
2 tbsp tomato purée
1½ tsp sugar
1 bay leaf
salt and pepper

 Serves 6

 Preparation time: 25 minutes,
plus 20 minutes pre-cooking

 Cooking time: 3–4 hours

---

1. First make the tomato sauce. Heat the oil in a heavy-based saucepan. Add the onions and cook over a medium heat, stirring occasionally, for 5 minutes until softened. Stir in the garlic and cook for 1 minute, then add the tomatoes, tomato purée, sugar and bay leaf. Season with salt and pepper and bring to the boil. Lower the heat and simmer gently for 20 minutes until thickened.

2. Meanwhile, mix together the nuts, onions, garlic, celery, cheese and thyme in a bowl. Lightly beat the eggs with the yeast extract in a jug, then stir into the nut mixture. Set aside.

3. Cut out the thick stalks from the cabbage leaves. Blanch the leaves in a large saucepan of boiling water for 5 minutes, then drain and refresh under cold water. Pat dry with kitchen paper.

4. Place a little of the nut mixture on the stalk end of each cabbage leaf. Fold the sides over, then roll up to make a neat parcel.

5. Arrange the parcels in the slow cooker, seam side down. Remove and discard the bay leaf from the tomato sauce and pour the sauce over the cabbage rolls. Cover and cook on low for 3–4 hours. Serve the cabbage roulades hot or cold.

Everyday Meals

Nothing is nicer on a cold winter evening than sitting down to this hearty traditional American one-pot dish.

Chicken Stew

Ingredients

3 tbsp sunflower oil

1 large onion, thinly sliced

1 green pepper, deseeded and chopped

8 chicken pieces, such as thighs and
   drumsticks

400 g/14 oz canned chopped tomatoes,
   drained

1 tbsp Worcestershire sauce

300 ml/10 fl oz hot chicken stock

1 tbsp cornflour

200 g/7 oz frozen sweetcorn, thawed

450 g/1 lb frozen broad beans, thawed

salt and cayenne pepper

crusty bread, to serve

 Serves 4

 Preparation time: 20 minutes,
plus 10 minutes pre-cooking

 Cooking time: 7 hours

---

1. Heat the oil in a large, heavy-based frying pan. Add the onion and pepper and cook over a medium heat, stirring occasionally, for 5 minutes until the onion is softened. Using a slotted spoon, transfer the mixture to the slow cooker.

2. Add the chicken to the pan and cook, turning occasionally, for 5 minutes until golden all over. Transfer to the slow cooker and add the tomatoes. Season with a pinch of cayenne pepper and salt. Stir the Worcestershire sauce into the hot stock and pour into the slow cooker. Cover and cook on low for 6½ hours.

3. Mix the cornflour to a paste with 2–3 tablespoons of water and stir into the stew. Add the sweetcorn and beans, re-cover and cook on high for 30–40 minutes until everything is cooked through and piping hot. Transfer to warm bowls and serve with crusty bread.

This is a classic Northern European combination that is traditionally served in the winter when red cabbage is in season.

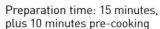

Chicken Braised with Red Cabbage

Ingredients

2 tbsp sunflower oil

4 skinless chicken thighs or drumsticks

1 onion, chopped

500 g/1 lb 2 oz red cabbage, cored
 and shredded

2 apples, peeled and chopped

12 canned or cooked chestnuts,
 halved (optional)

½ tsp juniper berries

125 ml/4 fl oz red wine

salt and pepper

fresh flat-leaf parsley, to garnish

Serves 4

Preparation time: 15 minutes,
plus 10 minutes pre-cooking

Cooking time: 5 hours

---

1. Heat the oil in a large, heavy-based saucepan. Add the chicken and cook, turning frequently, for 5 minutes until golden on all sides. Using a slotted spoon transfer to a plate lined with kitchen paper.

2. Add the onion to the saucepan and cook over a medium heat, stirring occasionally, until softened. Stir in the cabbage and apples and cook, stirring occasionally, for 5 minutes. Add the chestnuts, if using, juniper berries and wine and season to taste with salt and pepper. Bring to the boil.

3. Spoon half the cabbage mixture into the slow cooker, add the chicken pieces, then top with the remaining cabbage mixture. Cover and cook on low for 5 hours until the chicken is tender and cooked through. Serve immediately, garnished with the parsley.

This colourful dish is perfect for a family dinner in the early spring, when the days are growing longer but the evenings are still cool. Serve with plain boiled rice or crusty bread.

Chicken with Red Pepper & Broad Beans

Ingredients

1½ tbsp plain flour

4 chicken portions, about 175 g/6 oz each

2 tbsp olive oil

1 onion, chopped

2–3 garlic cloves, chopped

1 fresh red chilli, deseeded and chopped

225 g/8 oz chorizo or other spicy sausages, skinned and cut into small chunks

300 ml/10 fl oz chicken stock

150 ml/5 fl oz dry white wine

1 tbsp dark soy sauce

1 large red pepper, deseeded and sliced into rings

225 g/8 oz shelled broad beans

25 g/1 oz rocket or baby spinach leaves

salt and pepper

 Serves 4

 Preparation time: 20 minutes, plus 20 minutes pre-cooking

 Cooking time: 7¼–7½ hours

1. Spread out the flour on a plate and season well with salt and pepper. Toss the chicken in the flour until thoroughly coated, shaking off any excess. Reserve any remaining flour.

2. Heat half the oil in a heavy-based frying pan, add the chicken portions and cook over a medium–high heat, turning frequently, for 10 minutes, or until golden brown all over. Add a little more oil during cooking if necessary. Using a slotted spoon, transfer the chicken to the slow cooker.

3. Add the remaining oil to the frying pan. Add the onion, garlic and chilli and cook over a low heat, stirring occasionally, for 5 minutes, until softened. Add the chorizo and cook, stirring frequently, for a further 2 minutes. Sprinkle in the remaining flour and cook, stirring constantly, for 2 minutes, then remove the pan from the heat. Gradually stir in the stock, wine and soy sauce, then return the pan to the heat and bring to the boil, stirring constantly. Pour the onion mixture over the chicken, then cover and cook on low for 6½ hours.

4. Add the red pepper and beans to the slow cooker, re-cover and cook on high for 45–60 minutes, until the chicken and vegetables are cooked through and tender. Season to taste with salt and pepper. Stir in the rocket and leave to stand for 2 minutes, until just wilted, then serve.

This unusual combination of flavours is a great way to perk up chicken portions without taking up much time or blowing the household budget. Caramelized apple slices add a special touch.

Chicken & Apple Pot

Ingredients
1 tbsp olive oil
4 chicken portions, about 175 g/6 oz each
1 onion, chopped
2 celery sticks, coarsely chopped
1½ tbsp plain flour
300 ml/10 fl oz clear apple juice
150 ml/5 fl oz chicken stock
1 cooking apple, cored and cut into quarters
2 bay leaves
1–2 tsp clear honey
1 yellow pepper, deseeded and
   cut into chunks
salt and pepper

For the garnish
1 large or 2 medium eating apples, cored
   and sliced
1 tbsp butter, melted
2 tbsp Demerara sugar
1 tbsp chopped fresh mint

 Serves 4

 Preparation time: 15 minutes,
plus 20 minutes pre-cooking

 Cooking time: 7¼ hours

1. Heat the oil in a heavy-based frying pan. Add the chicken and cook over a medium–high heat, turning frequently, for 10 minutes, until golden brown all over. Using a slotted spoon, transfer the chicken to the slow cooker.

2. Add the onion and celery to the pan and cook over a low heat, stirring occasionally, for 5 minutes until softened. Sprinkle in the flour and cook, stirring constantly, for 2 minutes, then remove the pan from the heat. Gradually stir in the apple juice and stock, then return the pan to the heat and bring to the boil, stirring constantly. Stir in the cooking apple, bay leaves and honey and season to taste with salt and pepper.

3. Pour the mixture over the chicken, cover the slow cooker and cook on low for 6½ hours, until the chicken is tender and the juices run clear when the thickest part is pierced with the point of a sharp knife. Stir in the yellow pepper, re-cover and cook on high for 45 minutes.

4. Shortly before you are ready to serve, preheat the grill. Brush one side of the apple slices with half the melted butter and sprinkle them with half the sugar. Grill for 2–3 minutes until the sugar has caramelized. Turn the slices over with tongs, brush with the remaining butter and sprinkle with the remaining sugar. Grill for a further 2 minutes. Serve the stew garnished with the caramelized apple slices and the mint.

This traditional European dish partners chicken and mushrooms with red wine, and the wine gives the onions in particular a delicious rich flavour.

Chicken & Mushroom Stew

Ingredients

15 g/½ oz unsalted butter

2 tbsp olive oil

1.8 kg/4 lb skinless chicken portions

2 red onions, sliced

2 garlic cloves, finely chopped

400 g/14 oz canned chopped tomatoes

2 tbsp chopped fresh flat-leaf parsley

6 fresh basil leaves, torn

1 tbsp sun-dried tomato purée

150 ml/5 fl oz red wine

225 g/8 oz mushrooms, sliced

salt and pepper

 Serves 4

 Preparation time: 10 minutes, plus 25 minutes pre-cooking

 Cooking time: 7 hours

---

1. Heat the butter and oil in a heavy-based frying pan. Add the chicken, in batches if necessary, and cook over a medium–high heat, turning frequently, for 10 minutes, until golden brown all over. Using a slotted spoon, transfer the chicken to the slow cooker.

2. Add the onions and garlic to the frying pan and cook over a low heat, stirring occasionally, for 10 minutes, until golden. Add the tomatoes with their can juices, stir in the parsley, basil, tomato purée and wine and season with salt and pepper. Bring to the boil, then pour the mixture over the chicken.

3. Cover the slow cooker and cook on low for 6½ hours. Stir in the mushrooms, re-cover and cook on high for 30 minutes, until the chicken is tender and the vegetables are cooked through. Taste and adjust the seasoning if necessary and serve.

Warming spices give this rich dish a delicious and unusual flavour that is sure to please a hungry family on a cold winter day.

Thick Beef & Button Onion Stew

Ingredients

2 tbsp olive oil

450 g/1 lb button onions, peeled but left whole

2 garlic cloves, halved

900 g/2 lb stewing beef, cubed

½ tsp ground cinnamon

1 tsp ground cloves

1 tsp ground cumin

2 tbsp tomato purée

1 bottle (750 ml) red wine

grated rind and juice of 1 orange

1 bay leaf

salt and pepper

1 tbsp chopped fresh flat-leaf parsley,
   to garnish

boiled potatoes, to serve

 Serves 6

 Preparation time: 20 minutes,
plus 15 minutes pre-cooking

 Cooking time: 9 hours

1. Heat the oil in a heavy frying pan. Add the onions and garlic and cook over a medium heat, stirring frequently, for 5 minutes until softened and beginning to brown. Increase the heat to high, add the beef and cook, stirring frequently, for 5 minutes, until browned all over.

2. Stir in the cinnamon, cloves, cumin and tomato purée and season with salt and pepper. Pour in the wine, scraping up any sediment from the base of the frying pan. Stir in the orange rind and juice, add the bay leaf and bring to the boil.

3. Transfer the mixture to the slow cooker, cover and cook on low for 9 hours, until the beef is tender. If possible, stir the stew once during the second half of the cooking time.

4. Serve the stew garnished with the parsley and accompanied by boiled potatoes.

This is an ideal dish for busy people as it contains everything you need for a filling and healthy meal, so there is no need to prepare any accompaniments.

Beef & Vegetable Stew with Corn

Ingredients

1½ tbsp plain flour

1 tsp hot paprika

1–1½ tsp chilli powder

1 tsp ground ginger

450 g/1 lb stewing steak, cubed

2 tbsp olive oil

1 large onion, cut into chunks

3 garlic cloves, sliced

2 celery sticks, sliced

225 g/8 oz carrots, chopped

300 ml/10 fl oz lager

300 ml/10 fl oz beef stock

350 g/12 oz potatoes, chopped

2 corn on the cobs, halved

1 red pepper, deseeded and chopped

115 g/4 oz tomatoes, cut into quarters

115 g/4 oz shelled peas, thawed if frozen

1 tbsp chopped fresh coriander

salt and pepper

 Serves 4

 Preparation time: 20 minutes, plus 12 minutes pre-cooking

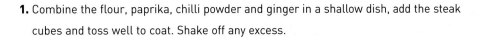 Cooking time: 9¼ hours

---

1. Combine the flour, paprika, chilli powder and ginger in a shallow dish, add the steak cubes and toss well to coat. Shake off any excess.

2. Heat the oil in a heavy-based frying pan. Add the onion, garlic and celery and cook over a low heat, stirring occasionally, for 5 minutes, until softened. Increase the heat to high, add the steak and cook, stirring frequently, for 3 minutes until browned all over. Add the carrots and remove the pan from the heat.

3. Gradually stir in the lager and stock, return the frying pan to the heat and bring to the boil, stirring constantly. Transfer the mixture to the slow cooker, add the potatoes and corn on the cobs, cover and cook on low for 8½ hours.

4. Add the red pepper, tomatoes and peas, re-cover and cook on high for 45 minutes, until the meat is tender and the vegetables are cooked through. Taste and adjust the seasoning if necessary, sprinkle with the coriander and serve.

This dish originated in Provence in the south of France where it is usually served with buttered noodles. It is equally good with a mound of hot mashed potatoes.

Beef Stew with Olives

Ingredients

900 g/2 lb stewing steak, cubed

2 onions, thinly sliced

2 carrots, sliced

4 large garlic cloves, lightly crushed

1 bouquet garni

4 juniper berries

500 ml/18 fl oz dry red wine

2 tbsp brandy

2 tbsp olive oil

3 tbsp plain flour

175 g/6 oz lardons or diced bacon

2 x 10-cm/4-inch strips of thinly pared
    orange rind

85 g/3 oz stoned black olives, rinsed

salt and pepper

tagliatelle or buttered noodles, to serve

To garnish

1 tbsp chopped fresh flat-leaf parsley

finely grated orange rind

 Serves 4–6

 Preparation time: 20 minutes,
plus 24 hours marinating

 Cooking time: 9½–10 hours

1. Put the stewing steak in a large, non-metallic dish, add the onions, carrots, garlic, bouquet garni and juniper berries and season with salt and pepper. Combine the wine, brandy and olive oil in a jug and pour the mixture over the meat and vegetables. Cover with clingfilm and marinate in the refrigerator for 24 hours.

2. Using a slotted spoon, remove the steak from the marinade and pat dry with kitchen paper. Reserve the marinade, vegetables and flavourings. Place the flour in a shallow dish and season well with salt and pepper. Toss the steak cubes in the flour until well coated and shake off any excess.

3. Sprinkle half the lardons in the base of the slow cooker and top with the steak cubes. Pour in the marinade, including the vegetables and flavourings, and add the strips of orange rind and the olives. Top with the remaining lardons. Cover and cook on low for 9½–10 hours, until the steak and vegetables are tender.

4. Remove and discard the bouquet garni and skim off any fat that has risen to the surface of the stew. Sprinkle the parsley and grated orange rind over the top and serve with tagliatelle or buttered noodles.

There are many versions of this traditional beef stew, which dates back to the ninth century. Finishing it with soured cream is, however, a modern addition.

Goulash

Ingredients

4 tbsp sunflower oil

650 g/1 lb 7 oz braising steak,
   cut into 2.5-cm/1-inch cubes

2 tsp plain flour

2 tsp paprika

300 ml/10 fl oz beef stock

3 onions, chopped

4 carrots, diced

1 large potato or 2 medium potatoes,
   diced

1 bay leaf

½–1 tsp caraway seeds

400 g/14 oz canned chopped tomatoes

2 tbsp soured cream

salt and pepper

 Serves 4

 Preparation time: 20 minutes,
   plus 25 minutes pre-cooking

 Cooking time: 9 hours

---

1. Heat half the oil in a heavy-based frying pan. Add the beef and cook over a medium heat, stirring frequently, until browned all over. Lower the heat and stir in the flour and paprika. Cook, stirring constantly, for 2 minutes. Gradually stir in the stock and bring to the boil, then transfer the mixture to the slow cooker.

2. Rinse out the frying pan and heat the remaining oil in it. Add the onions and cook over a low heat, stirring occasionally, for 5 minutes until softened. Stir in the carrots and potato and cook for a few minutes more. Add the bay leaf, caraway seeds and tomatoes with their can juices. Season with salt and pepper.

3. Transfer the vegetable mixture to the slow cooker, stir well, then cover and cook on low for 9 hours until the meat is tender.

4. Remove and discard the bay leaf. Pour over the soured cream and serve immediately.

Lamb Stew with Red Peppers brings a hint of exotic North African cooking to the dinner table with this subtly spiced, succulent lamb stew flavoured with orange juice.

Lamb Stew with Red Peppers

Ingredients

1½ tbsp plain flour

1 tsp ground cloves

450 g/1 lb boneless lamb, cut into thin strips

1–1½ tbsp olive oil

1 white onion, sliced

2–3 garlic cloves, sliced

300 ml/10 fl oz orange juice

150 ml/5 fl oz lamb or chicken stock

1 cinnamon stick

2 red peppers, deseeded and
    sliced into rings

4 tomatoes

4 fresh coriander sprigs

salt and pepper

1 tbsp chopped fresh coriander, to garnish

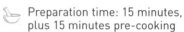

To serve

mashed sweet potatoes mixed with
    chopped spring onions

green vegetables

🍲 Serves 4

🥣 Preparation time: 15 minutes,
    plus 15 minutes pre-cooking

🧤 Cooking time: 7–8 hours

---

1. Combine the flour and ground cloves in a shallow dish, add the strips of lamb and toss well to coat, shaking off any excess. Reserve the remaining spiced flour.

2. Heat 1 tbsp of the oil in a heavy-based frying pan, add the lamb and cook over a high heat, stirring frequently, for 3 minutes, until browned all over. Using a slotted spoon, transfer the lamb to the slow cooker.

3. Add the onion and garlic to the frying pan, with the remaining oil if necessary, and cook over a low heat, stirring occasionally, for 5 minutes, until softened. Sprinkle in the reserved spiced flour and cook, stirring constantly, for 2 minutes, then remove the pan from the heat. Gradually stir in the orange juice and stock, then return the pan to the heat and bring to the boil, stirring constantly.

4. Pour the mixture over the lamb, add the cinnamon stick, red peppers, tomatoes and coriander sprigs and stir well. Cover and cook on low for 7–8 hours until the meat is tender.

5. Remove and discard the cinnamon stick and coriander sprigs. Season to taste with salt and pepper, sprinkle the stew with chopped coriander and serve with mashed sweet potatoes with spring onions and green vegetables.

It is worth buying good-quality gammon for this traditional, country-style American dish as the flavour and texture are infinitely superior.

Ham with Black-Eyed Beans

Ingredients
550 g/1 lb 4 oz lean gammon
2–3 tbsp olive oil
1 onion, chopped
2–3 garlic cloves, chopped
2 celery sticks, chopped
175 g/6 oz carrots, thinly sliced
1 cinnamon stick
½ tsp ground cloves
¼ tsp freshly grated nutmeg
1 tsp dried oregano
450 ml/16 fl oz chicken or vegetable stock
2 tbsp maple syrup
225 g/8 oz chorizo or other spicy sausages, skinned
400 g/14 oz canned black-eyed beans, drained and rinsed
1 orange pepper, deseeded and chopped
1 tbsp cornflour
pepper
fresh flat-leaf parsley or oregano sprig, to garnish

 Serves 4

 Preparation time: 20 minutes, plus 15 minutes pre-cooking

 Cooking time: 6¼–7¾ hours

1. Trim off any fat from the gammon and cut the flesh into 4-cm/1½-inch pieces. Heat 1 tbsp of the oil in a heavy-based frying pan, add the gammon and cook over a high heat, stirring frequently, for 5 minutes until browned all over. Using a slotted spoon, transfer the gammon to the slow cooker.

2. Add 1 tbsp of the remaining oil to the frying pan. Reduce the heat to low, add the onion, garlic, celery and carrots and cook, stirring occasionally, for 5 minutes until softened. Add the cinnamon, cloves and nutmeg, season with pepper and cook, stirring constantly, for 2 minutes. Stir in the dried oregano, stock and maple syrup and bring to the boil, stirring constantly. Pour the mixture over the gammon, stir well, cover and cook on low for 5–6 hours.

3. Heat the remaining oil in a frying pan, add the chorizo and cook, turning frequently, for 10 minutes until browned all over. Remove from the pan, cut each into 3–4 chunks and add to the slow cooker with the black-eyed beans and orange pepper. Re-cover and cook on high for 1–1½ hours.

4. Stir the cornflour with 2 tbsp water to a smooth paste in a small bowl, then stir into the stew, re-cover and cook on high for 15 minutes. Remove and discard the cinnamon stick, garnish the stew with a fresh herb sprig and serve.

This lovely summery dish is perfect for family suppers and is special enough to serve to guests.

Tagliatelle with Prawns

Ingredients

400 g/14 oz tomatoes, peeled and chopped
140 g/5 oz tomato purée
1 garlic clove, finely chopped
2 tbsp chopped fresh parsley
500 g/1 lb 2 oz cooked, peeled
   Mediterranean prawns
6 fresh basil leaves, torn
400 g/14 oz dried tagliatelle
salt and pepper
fresh basil leaves, to garnish

 Serves 4
 Preparation time: 10 minutes
 Cooking time: 7¼ hours

1. Put the tomatoes, tomato purée, garlic and parsley in the slow cooker and season with salt and pepper. Cover and cook on low for 7 hours.

2. Add the prawns and basil. Re-cover and cook on high for 15 minutes.

3. Meanwhile, bring a large saucepan of lightly salted water to the boil. Add the pasta, bring back to the boil and cook for 10–12 minutes until tender but still firm to the bite.

4. Drain the pasta and tip it into a warm serving bowl. Add the prawn sauce and toss lightly with 2 large forks. Garnish with the basil leaves and serve immediately.

This famous southern stew gets its name from the West African name for okra-gumbo – a vegetable that not only provides flavour but helps to thicken it.

Louisiana Gumbo

Ingredients

2 tbsp sunflower oil

175 g/6 oz okra, trimmed and
   cut into 2.5-cm/1-inch pieces

2 onions, finely chopped

4 celery sticks, very finely chopped

1 garlic clove, finely chopped

2 tbsp plain flour

½ tsp sugar

1 tsp ground cumin

700ml/1¼ pints fish stock

1 red pepper, deseeded and chopped

1 green pepper, deseeded and chopped

2 large tomatoes, chopped

4 tbsp chopped fresh parsley

1 tbsp chopped fresh coriander

dash of Tabasco

350 g/12 oz large raw prawns, peeled and
   deveined

350 g/12 oz cod or haddock fillets, skinned
   and cut into 2.5-cm/1-inch chunks

350 g/12 oz monkfish fillet,
   cut into 2.5-cm/1-inch chunks

salt and pepper

 Serves 6

 Preparation time: 30 minutes,
plus 15 minutes pre-cooking

 Cooking time: 5½–6½ hours

---

1. Heat half the oil in a heavy-based frying pan. Add the okra and cook over a low heat, stirring frequently, for 5 minutes until browned. Using a slotted spoon, transfer the okra to the slow cooker.

2. Add the remaining oil to the frying pan. Add the onions and celery and cook over a low heat, stirring occasionally, for 5 minutes until softened. Add the garlic and cook, stirring frequently, for 1 minute, then sprinkle in the flour, sugar and cumin and season with salt and pepper. Cook, stirring constantly, for 2 minutes, then remove the frying pan from the heat.

3. Gradually stir in the stock, then return the pan to the heat and bring to the boil, stirring constantly. Pour the mixture over the okra and stir in the peppers and tomatoes. Cover and cook on low for 5–6 hours.

4. Stir in the parsley, coriander and Tabasco to taste, then add the prawns, cod and monkfish. Cover and cook on high for 30 minutes until the fish is cooked and the prawns have changed colour. Taste and adjust the seasoning if necessary and serve.

Peppers, tomatoes, chillies, garlic and herbs give this seafood medley a fabulous depth of flavour and a colourful appearance.

South-western Seafood Stew

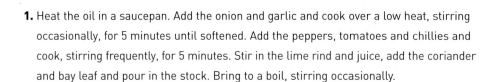

Ingredients

2 tbsp olive oil, plus extra for drizzling

1 large onion, chopped

4 garlic cloves, finely chopped

1 yellow pepper, peeled, deseeded and chopped

1 red pepper, peeled, deseeded and chopped

1 orange pepper, peeled, deseeded and chopped

450 g/1 lb tomatoes, peeled and chopped

2 large, mild green chillies, such as poblano, chopped

finely grated rind and juice of 1 lime

2 tbsp chopped fresh coriander, plus extra leaves to garnish

1 bay leaf

450 ml/16 fl oz fish, vegetable or chicken stock

450 g/1 lb red mullet fillets

450 g/1 lb raw prawns

225 g/8 oz prepared squid

salt and pepper

Serves 4

Preparation time: 20 minutes, plus 15 minutes pre-cooking

Cooking time: 8 hours

---

1. Heat the oil in a saucepan. Add the onion and garlic and cook over a low heat, stirring occasionally, for 5 minutes until softened. Add the peppers, tomatoes and chillies and cook, stirring frequently, for 5 minutes. Stir in the lime rind and juice, add the coriander and bay leaf and pour in the stock. Bring to a boil, stirring occasionally.

2. Transfer the mixture to the slow cooker, cover and cook on low for 7½ hours. Meanwhile, skin the fish fillets, if necessary, and cut the flesh into chunks. Shell and devein the prawns. Cut the squid bodies into rings and halve the tentacles or leave them whole.

3. Add the seafood to the stew, season with salt and pepper, re-cover and cook on high for 30 minutes, or until tender and cooked through. Remove and discard the bay leaf, garnish the stew with coriander leaves and serve.

This fabulous vegetarian dish, based on the new season's fresh, young vegetables, is guaranteed to become a favourite even among meat-eaters.

Spring Stew

Ingredients

2 tbsp olive oil

4–8 baby onions, halved

2 celery sticks, cut into 5-mm/¼-inch slices

225 g/8 oz young carrots, halved if large

300 g/10½ oz new potatoes, halved

850 ml–1.2 litres/1½–2 pints vegetable stock

225 g/8 oz dried haricot beans, soaked
  overnight in cold water and drained

1 bouquet garni

1½–2 tbsp light soy sauce

85 g/3 oz baby sweetcorn

115 g/4 oz shelled broad beans,
  thawed if frozen

225 g/8 oz Savoy cabbage, shredded

1½ tbsp cornflour

salt and pepper

55–85 g/2–3 oz Parmesan cheese, freshly
  grated, to serve

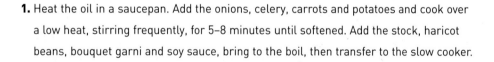

 Serves 4

 Preparation time: 15 minutes,
plus overnight soaking,
plus 10–12 minutes pre-cooking

 Cooking time: 3¼–4¼ hours

1. Heat the oil in a saucepan. Add the onions, celery, carrots and potatoes and cook over a low heat, stirring frequently, for 5–8 minutes until softened. Add the stock, haricot beans, bouquet garni and soy sauce, bring to the boil, then transfer to the slow cooker.

2. Add the corn, broad beans and cabbage, season with salt and pepper and stir well. Cover and cook on high for 3–4 hours until the vegetables are tender.

3. Remove and discard the bouquet garni. Stir the cornflour with 3 tbsp water to a paste in a small bowl, then stir into the stew. Re-cover and cook on high for a further 15 minutes until thickened. Serve the stew with the Parmesan.

Entertaining

There is something almost magical about coming home on a cold day to a tender beef pot roast and all its accompanying vegetables.

Traditional Pot Roast

Ingredients

1 onion, finely chopped
4 carrots, sliced
4 baby turnips, sliced
4 celery sticks, sliced
2 potatoes, peeled and sliced
1 sweet potato, peeled and sliced
1.3–1.8 kg/3–4 lb topside of beef
1 bouquet garni
300 ml/10 fl oz hot beef stock
salt and pepper
fresh thyme sprig, to garnish

 Serves 6
 Preparation time: 20 minutes
Cooking time: 9–10 hours

1. Place the onion, carrots, turnips, celery, potatoes and sweet potato in the slow cooker and stir to mix well.

2. Rub the beef all over with salt and pepper, then place on top of the bed of vegetables. Add the bouquet garni and pour in the stock. Cover and cook on low for 9–10 hours until the beef is cooked to your liking.

3. Remove the beef, carve into slices and arrange on serving plates. Remove and discard the bouquet garni. Spoon the vegetables and cooking juices onto the plates and serve.

As the duckling is braised gently, all the meat becomes deliciously tender, so you can use the whole bird for this tasty French dish.

Duckling with Apples

Ingredients

1.8–2 kg/4–4 lb 8 oz duckling,
    cut into 8 pieces
2 tbsp olive oil
1 onion, finely chopped
1 carrot, finely chopped
300 ml/10 fl oz chicken stock
300 ml/10 fl oz dry white wine
bouquet garni
4 eating apples
55 g/2 oz unsalted butter
salt and pepper

 Serves 4

 Preparation time: 15 minutes,
plus 15 minutes pre-cooking,
plus 5 minutes to finish

 Cooking time: 8 hours

1. Season the duckling pieces with salt and pepper. Heat the oil in a large, heavy-based frying pan. Add all the duckling pieces, placing the breast portions skin side down. Cook over a medium–high heat for a few minutes until golden brown, then transfer the breast portions to a plate. Turn the other pieces and continue to cook until browned all over. Transfer to the plate.

2. Add the onion and carrot to the frying pan and cook over a low heat, stirring occasionally, for 5 minutes until the onion is softened. Add the stock and wine and bring to the boil.

3. Transfer the vegetable mixture to the slow cooker. Add the duckling pieces and the bouquet garni. Cover and cook on low for 8 hours, occasionally skimming off the fat from the slow cooker and replacing the lid immediately each time.

4. Shortly before you are ready to serve, peel, core and slice the apples. Melt the butter in a large frying pan. Add the apple slices and cook over a medium heat, turning occasionally, for 6 minutes until golden.

5. Spoon the cooked apples onto warmed plates and divide the duckling among them. Skim off the fat and strain the sauce into a jug, then pour it over the duckling and serve.

This North African combination of lamb, dried fruit and nuts is delicately spiced and wonderfully rich in flavour.

Lamb Tagine

Ingredients
3 tbsp olive oil

2 red onions, chopped

2 garlic cloves, finely chopped

2.5-cm/1-inch piece fresh root ginger, finely chopped

1 yellow pepper, deseeded and chopped

1 kg/2 lb 4 oz boneless shoulder of lamb, trimmed and cut into 2.5-cm/1-inch cubes

850 ml/1½ pints lamb or chicken stock

225 g/8 oz ready-to-eat dried apricots, halved

1 tbsp clear honey

4 tbsp lemon juice

pinch of saffron threads

5-cm/2-inch cinnamon stick

salt and pepper

To garnish
55 g/2 oz flaked almonds, toasted

fresh coriander sprigs

 Serves 6

 Preparation time: 15 minutes, plus 10 minutes pre-cooking

 Cooking time: 8½ hours

---

1. Heat the oil in a large, heavy-based saucepan. Add the onions, garlic, ginger and yellow pepper and cook over a low heat, stirring occasionally, for 5 minutes until the onion has softened. Add the lamb and stir well to mix, then pour in the stock. Add the apricots, honey, lemon juice, saffron and cinnamon stick and season with the salt and pepper. Bring to the boil.

2. Transfer the mixture to the slow cooker. Cover and cook on low for 8½ hours until the meat is tender.

3. Remove and discard the cinnamon stick. Transfer to warmed serving bowls, sprinkle with the almonds, garnish with fresh coriander and serve.

Seasonal ingredients have a deliciously fresh flavour, but you can enjoy the taste of springtime at any time of year if you use frozen asparagus.

Springtime Lamb with Asparagus

Ingredients

2 tbsp sunflower oil

1 onion, thinly sliced

2 garlic cloves, very finely chopped

1 kg/2 lb 4 oz boneless shoulder of lamb,
　　cut into 2.5-cm/1-in cubes

225 g/8 oz asparagus spears, thawed if frozen

300 ml/10 fl oz chicken stock

4 tbsp lemon juice

150 ml/5 fl oz double cream

salt and pepper

 Serves 6

 Preparation time: 20 minutes,
plus 10 minutes pre-cooking,
plus 5 minutes to finish

Cooking time: 7¼ hours

1. Heat the oil in a large, heavy-based frying pan. Add the onion and cook over a medium heat, stirring occasionally, for 5 minutes until softened. Add the garlic and lamb and cook, stirring occasionally, for a further 5 minutes until the lamb is lightly browned all over.

2. Meanwhile, trim off and reserve the tips of the asparagus spears. Cut the stalks into 2–3 pieces. Add the stock and lemon juice to the frying pan, season with salt and pepper and bring to the boil. Lower the heat, add the asparagus stalks and simmer for 2 minutes.

3. Transfer the mixture to the slow cooker. Cover and cook on low for 7 hours until the lamb is tender.

4. About 20 minutes before you intend to serve, cook the reserved asparagus tips in a saucepan of lightly salted boiling water for 5 minutes. Drain well, then mix with the cream. Spoon the cream mixture on top of the lamb mixture but do not stir it in. Re-cover and cook on high for 15–20 minutes to heat through before serving.

This is the perfect choice for slow cooking as the meat becomes melt-in-the-mouth tender and the flavours mingle superbly.

Lamb Shanks with Olives

Ingredients

1½ tbsp plain flour

4 lamb shanks

2 tbsp olive oil

1 onion, sliced

2 garlic cloves, finely chopped

2 tsp sweet paprika

400 g/14 oz canned chopped tomatoes

2 tbsp tomato purée

2 carrots, sliced

2 tsp sugar

225 ml/8 fl oz red wine

5-cm/2-inch cinnamon stick

2 fresh rosemary sprigs

115 g/4 oz stoned black olives

2 tbsp lemon juice

2 tbsp chopped fresh mint

salt and pepper

fresh mint leaves, to garnish

   Serves 4

Preparation time: 15 minutes, plus 15 minutes pre-cooking

Cooking time: 8½ hours

---

1. Spread out the flour on a plate and season with salt and pepper. Toss the lamb in the seasoned flour and shake off any excess. Heat the oil in a large, heavy-based saucepan. Add the lamb shanks and cook over a medium heat, turning frequently, for 6–8 minutes until browned all over. Transfer to a plate and set aside.

2. Add the onions and garlic to the saucepan and cook, stirring frequently, for 5 minutes until softened. Stir in the paprika and cook for 1 minute. Add the tomatoes, tomato purée, carrots, sugar, wine, cinnamon stick and rosemary and bring to the boil.

3. Transfer the vegetable mixture to the slow cooker and add the lamb shanks. Cover and cook on low for 8 hours until the lamb is very tender.

4. Add the olives, lemon juice and mint to the slow cooker. Re-cover and cook on high for 30 minutes. Remove and discard the rosemary and cinnamon and serve, garnished with mint leaves.

Olives, chillies, capers and, of course, almonds, provide a delicious mix of flavours in this traditional Mexican stew.

Pork with Almonds

Ingredients

2 tbsp sunflower oil

2 onions, chopped

2 garlic cloves, finely chopped

5-cm/2-inch cinnamon stick

3 cloves

115 g/4 oz ground almonds

750 g/1 lb 10 oz boneless pork,
    cut into 2.5-cm/1-inch cubes

4 tomatoes, peeled and chopped

2 tbsp capers

115 g/4 oz green olives, stoned

3 pickled jalapeño chillies, drained,
    deseeded and cut into rings

350 ml/12 fl oz chicken stock

salt and pepper

fresh coriander sprigs, to garnish (optional)

 Serves 4

 Preparation time: 25 minutes,
plus 25 minutes pre-cooking

 Cooking time: 5 hours

---

1. Heat half the oil in a large, heavy-based frying pan. Add the onions and cook over a low heat, stirring occasionally, for 5 minutes until softened. Add the garlic, cinnamon, cloves and almonds and cook, stirring frequently, for 8–10 minutes. Be careful not to burn the almonds.

2. Remove and discard the spices and transfer the mixture to a food processor. Process to a smooth purée.

3. Rinse out the pan and return to the heat. Heat the remaining oil, then add the pork, in batches if necessary. Cook over a medium heat, stirring frequently, for 5–10 minutes until browned all over. Return all the pork to the pan and add the almond purée, tomatoes, capers, olives, chillies and chicken stock. Bring to the boil, then transfer to the slow cooker.

4. Season with salt and pepper and mix well. Cover and cook on low for 5 hours. To serve, transfer to warmed plates and garnish with coriander sprigs, if desired.

In this recipe, chicken simmers to tender perfection in a rich sauce flavoured with walnuts, lemon, ginger and, surprisingly, black treacle.

Nutty Chicken

Ingredients

3 tbsp sunflower oil

4 skinless chicken portions

2 shallots, chopped

1 tsp ground ginger

1 tbsp plain flour

425 ml/15 fl oz beef stock

55 g/2 oz walnut pieces

grated rind of 1 lemon

2 tbsp lemon juice

1 tbsp black treacle

salt and pepper

fresh watercress sprigs, to garnish

 Serves 4

 Preparation time: 15 minutes, plus 10–15 minutes pre-cooking

 Cooking time: 6 hours

---

1. Heat the oil in a large, heavy-based frying pan. Season the chicken portions with salt and pepper and add to the pan. Cook over a medium heat, turning occasionally, for 5–8 minutes until lightly golden all over. Transfer to the slow cooker.

2. Add the shallots to the pan and cook, stirring occasionally, for 3–4 minutes until softened. Sprinkle in the ginger and flour and cook, stirring constantly, for 1 minute. Gradually stir in the stock and bring to the boil, stirring constantly. Lower the heat and simmer for 1 minute, then stir in the nuts, lemon rind and juice and treacle.

3. Pour the sauce over the chicken. Cover and cook on low for 6 hours until the chicken is cooked through and tender. Taste and adjust the seasoning if necessary. Transfer the chicken to warm bowls, spoon some of the sauce over each portion, garnish with watercress sprigs and serve immediately.

This is a great way to cook a gammon joint as it prevents the meat from drying out and allows the delicious spicy flavours to penetrate.

Gammon Cooked in Cider

Ingredients

1 kg/2 lb 4 oz boneless gammon joint

1 onion, halved

4 cloves

6 black peppercorns

1 tsp juniper berries

1 celery stick, chopped

1 carrot, sliced

1 litre/1¾ pints medium cider

fresh vegetables, such as mashed
    potatoes and peas, to serve

Serves 6

Preparation time: 10 minutes,
plus 15 minutes standing

Cooking time: 8 hours

1. Place a trivet or rack in the slow cooker, if you like, and stand the gammon on it.
   Otherwise, just place the gammon in the cooker. Stud each of the onion halves with
   2 cloves and add to the cooker with the peppercorns, juniper berries, celery and carrot.

2. Pour in the cider, cover and cook on low for 8 hours until the meat is tender.

3. Remove the gammon from the cooker and place on a board. Tent with foil and leave to
   stand for 10–15 minutes. Discard the cooking liquid and flavourings.

4. Cut off any rind and fat from the gammon joint, then carve into slices and serve with
   fresh vegetables.

Serve this traditional Italian dish with pasta, or a crisp mixed salad if you are following a low-carb diet.

Chicken Cacciatore

Ingredients

3 tbsp olive oil

4 chicken portions, skinned

2 onions, sliced

2 garlic cloves, finely chopped

400 g/14 oz canned chopped tomatoes

1 tbsp tomato purée

2 tbsp chopped fresh parsley

2 tsp fresh thyme leaves

150 ml/5 fl oz red wine

salt and pepper

fresh thyme sprigs, to garnish

 Serves 4

 Preparation time: 20 minutes, plus 15 minutes pre-cooking

 Cooking time: 5 hours

1. Heat the oil in a heavy-based frying pan. Add the chicken portions and cook over a medium heat, turning occasionally, for 10 minutes until golden all over. Using a slotted spoon, transfer the chicken to the slow cooker.

2. Add the onions to the pan and cook, stirring occasionally, for 5 minutes until softened and just turning golden. Add the garlic, tomatoes and their can juices, tomato purée, parsley, thyme and wine. Season with salt and pepper and bring to the boil.

3. Pour the tomato mixture over the chicken pieces. Cover and cook on low for 5 hours until the chicken is tender and cooked through. Taste and adjust the seasoning if necessary and serve, garnished with sprigs of thyme.

The musky, slightly honey flavour of this wine complements the chicken superbly and its steely edge cuts through the richness of the cream.

Chicken in Riesling

Ingredients

2 tbsp plain flour

1 chicken, about 1.6 kg/3 lb 8 oz,
  cut into 8 pieces

55 g/2 oz unsalted butter

1 tbsp sunflower oil

4 shallots, finely chopped

12 button mushrooms, sliced

2 tbsp brandy

500 ml/18 fl oz Riesling wine

250 ml/9 fl oz double cream

salt and pepper

chopped fresh flat-leaf parsley, to garnish

 Serves 4–6

 Preparation time: 20 minutes,
  plus 15 minutes pre-cooking,
  plus 5 minutes for the sauce

 Cooking time: 5–6 hours

1. Put the flour in a shallow dish and season with salt and pepper. Toss the chicken pieces in the flour until well coated and shake off any excess. Heat half the butter with the oil in a heavy-based frying pan. Add the chicken pieces and cook over a medium–high heat, turning frequently, for 10 minutes until golden all over. Using a slotted spoon, transfer them to a plate.

2. Pour off the fat from the frying pan and wipe the base with kitchen paper. Melt the remaining butter. Add the shallots and mushrooms and cook over a medium–high heat, stirring constantly, for 3 minutes until the shallots are golden and the mushrooms lightly browned. Return the chicken to the frying pan and remove it from the heat. Warm the brandy in a small ladle, ignite and pour it over the chicken, shaking the pan gently until the flames have died down.

3. Return the pan to the heat and pour in the wine. Bring to the boil over a low heat, scraping any sediment from the base of the pan. Transfer to the slow cooker, cover and cook on low for 5–6 hours until the chicken is tender.

4. Transfer the chicken to a serving dish and keep warm. Skim off any fat from the surface of the cooking liquid and pour the liquid into a saucepan. Stir in the cream and bring just to the boil over a low heat. Season to taste with salt and pepper and pour the sauce over the chicken. Sprinkle with chopped parsley and serve immediately.

Although thought of as a fatty meat, duckling can often be disappointingly dry but there's no fear of failure with this luscious and colourful stew.

Duckling & Red Wine Stew

Ingredients

4 duckling portions, about 175 g/6 oz each

1 red onion, cut into wedges

2–3 garlic cloves, chopped

1 large carrot, chopped

2 celery sticks, chopped

2 tbsp plain flour

300 ml/10 fl oz red wine

2 tbsp brandy

175 ml/6 fl oz chicken stock or water

7.5-cm/3-inch strip of thinly pared orange rind

2 tbsp redcurrant jelly

115 g/4 oz sugar snap peas

1–2 tsp olive oil

115 g/4 oz button mushrooms

salt and pepper

1 tbsp chopped fresh parsley, to garnish

 Serves 4

 Preparation time: 10 minutes, plus 15 minutes pre-cooking

 Cooking time: 8½ hours

1. Heat a heavy-based frying pan for 1 minute, then add the duckling portions and cook over a low heat until the fat runs. Increase the heat to medium and cook, turning once, for 5 minutes until browned on both sides. Using a slotted spoon, transfer to the slow cooker.

2. Add the onion, garlic, carrot and celery to the frying pan and cook, stirring occasionally, for 5 minutes until softened. Sprinkle in the flour and cook, stirring constantly, for 2 minutes, then remove the pan from the heat. Gradually stir in the wine, brandy and stock, return the pan to the heat and bring to the boil, stirring constantly. Season with salt and pepper and stir in the orange rind and redcurrant jelly. Pour the mixture over the duckling portions, cover and cook on low for 8 hours, occasionally skimming off the fat from the stew and replacing the lid of the slow cooker immediately each time.

3. Cook the sugar snaps in a pan of boiling water for 3 minutes, then drain. Heat the olive oil in another pan, add the mushrooms and cook, stirring frequently for 3 minutes. Add the sugar snaps and mushrooms to the stew, re-cover and cook on high for 25–30 minutes until tender. Serve garnished with the parsley.

Venison, the name for meat from a wide variety of deer, is easy to obtain these days and usually less expensive than beef. It is tasty, nutritious and low in fat.

Venison Casserole

Ingredients

3 tbsp olive oil

1 kg/2 lb 4 oz stewing venison, cut into
  3-cm/1¼-cm cubes

2 onions, thinly sliced

2 garlic cloves, chopped

350 ml/12 fl oz beef stock

2 tbsp plain flour

125 ml/4 fl oz port

2 tbsp redcurrant jelly

6 juniper berries, crushed

4 cloves, crushed

pinch of ground cinnamon

pinch of freshly grated nutmeg

salt and pepper

mashed potatoes, to serve

 Serves 6

Preparation time: 15 minutes,
plus 15 minutes pre-cooking

Cooking time: 7–8 hours

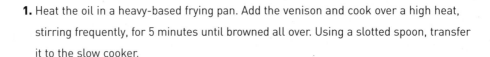

1. Heat the oil in a heavy-based frying pan. Add the venison and cook over a high heat, stirring frequently, for 5 minutes until browned all over. Using a slotted spoon, transfer it to the slow cooker.

2. Add the onions and garlic to the frying pan, lower the heat and cook, stirring occasionally, for 5 minutes until softened. Transfer them to the slow cooker.

3. Gradually stir the stock into the frying pan, scraping up any sediment from the base, then bring to the boil, stirring constantly. Sprinkle the flour over the meat in the slow cooker and stir well to coat evenly. Stir in the hot stock, then stir in the port, redcurrant, jelly, juniper berries, cloves, cinnamon and nutmeg. Season with salt and pepper. Cover and cook on low for 7–8 hours until the meat is tender.

4. Taste and adjust the seasoning if necessary. Remove and discard the cloves, then serve with mashed potatoes.

This elegant dish tastes fabulous and will be a sure-fire hit at any dinner party, yet it is surprisingly easy to prepare.

Seafood in Saffron Sauce

Ingredients

2 tbsp olive oil

1 onion, sliced

2 celery sticks, sliced

pinch of saffron threads

1 tbsp chopped fresh thyme

2 garlic cloves, finely chopped

800 g/1 lb 12 oz canned tomatoes, drained
  and chopped

175 ml/6 fl oz dry white wine

2 litres/3½ pints fish stock

225 g/8 oz live clams

225 g/8 oz live mussels

350 g/12 oz red mullet fillets

450 g/1 lb monkfish fillet

225 g/8 oz squid rings, thawed if frozen

2 tbsp shredded fresh basil leaves

salt and pepper

 Serves 4

 Preparation time: 10 minutes,
    plus 10 minutes pre-cooking

 Cooking time: 5 ½ hours

---

1. Heat the oil in a heavy-based frying pan. Add the onion, celery, saffron, thyme and a pinch of salt and cook over a low heat, stirring occasionally, for 5 minutes until softened. Add the garlic and cook, stirring constantly, for 2 minutes.

2. Add the tomatoes, wine and stock, season with salt and pepper and bring to the boil, stirring constantly. Transfer the mixture to the slow cooker, cover and cook on low for 5 hours.

3. Meanwhile, scrub the shellfish under cold running water and pull the 'beards' off the mussels. Discard any with broken shells or that do not shut immediately when sharply tapped. Cut the mullet and monkfish fillets into bite-size chunks.

4. Add the pieces of fish, the shellfish and the squid rings to the slow cooker, re-cover and cook on high for 30 minutes until the clams and mussels have opened and the fish is cooked through. Discard any shellfish that remain closed. Stir in the basil and serve.

Inspired by the cuisine of South-east Asia, this colourful and aromatic vegetarian medley would be a delightful treat for friends who don't eat meat.

Fragrant Vegetable Pot

Ingredients

3 tbsp groundnut oil

250 g/9 oz firm tofu, cut into bite-size cubes

2.5-cm/1-inch piece fresh root ginger, grated

2 lemongrass stalks, finely chopped

1–2 garlic cloves, crushed

1–2 bird's eye chillies, deseeded and chopped

3 celery sticks, sliced

3 shallots, cut into wedges

175 g/6 oz carrots, cut into batons

1 red pepper, deseeded and cut into chunks

1 yellow pepper, deseeded and cut into chunks

115 g/4 oz baby sweetcorn

1 tsp brown sugar

600 ml/1 pint vegetable stock

2 tbsp light soy sauce

1½ tbsp cornflour

115 g/4 oz French beans

85 g/3 oz broccoli, divided into florets

6 spring onions

1 tbsp chopped fresh coriander

pepper

jasmine rice, to serve

 Serves 4

 Preparation time: 20 minutes, plus 20 minutes pre-cooking

 Cooking time: 5¾–6 hours

---

1. Heat 2 tbsp of the oil in a heavy-based frying pan. Add the tofu and cook over a low heat, stirring frequently, for 8–10 minutes until golden brown all over. Using a slotted spoon, transfer to a plate and set aside.

2. Drain and wipe the frying pan with kitchen paper. Add the remaining oil and heat. Add the ginger, lemongrass, garlic and chillies and cook over a medium heat, stirring frequently, for 3 minutes. Add the celery and shallots and cook, stirring constantly, for 2 minutes, then add the carrots, peppers and baby sweetcorn. Sprinkle with the sugar, stir in the stock and soy sauce and bring to the boil, stirring. Transfer to the slow cooker, cover and cook on low for 5 hours.

3. Stir the cornflour with 3 tbsp water to a paste in a small bowl, then stir into the slow cooker. Add the beans, broccoli, spring onions, coriander and tofu, season with pepper and stir gently. Re-cover and cook on high for 45–60 minutes until all the vegetables are tender. Serve with jasmine rice.

It's hard to believe that the humble bean stew could become so glamorous and tasty as this marvellous mingling of flavours and textures.

Tuscan Bean Stew

Ingredients

1 large fennel bulb

2 tbsp olive oil

1 red onion, cut into small wedges

2–4 garlic cloves, sliced

1 green chilli, deseeded and chopped

1 aubergine, about 225 g/8 oz, cut into chunks

2 tbsp tomato purée

450 ml/16 fl oz vegetable stock

450 g/1 lb tomatoes

1 tbsp balsamic vinegar

4 fresh oregano sprigs

400 g/14 oz canned borlotti beans, drained and rinsed

400 g/14 oz canned flageolet beans, drained and rinsed

1 yellow pepper, deseeded and cut into small strips

1 courgette, halved lengthways and sliced

55 g/2 oz stoned black olives

salt and pepper

25 g/1 oz Parmesan cheese, to garnish

 Serves 4

 Preparation time: 20 minutes, plus 15–20 minutes pre-cooking

 Cooking time: 3–4 hours

---

1. Trim the fennel bulb, reserving the feathery fronds, then cut the bulb into thin strips. Heat the oil in a heavy-based frying pan. Add the fennel strips, onion, garlic and chilli and cook over a low heat, stirring occasionally, for 5–8 minutes until softened. Add the aubergine and cook, stirring frequently, for 5 minutes.

2. Mix together the tomato purée and half the stock in a jug and add to the frying pan. Pour in the remaining stock, add the tomatoes, vinegar and oregano and bring to the boil, stirring constantly.

3. Transfer the mixture to the slow cooker. Stir in the beans, pepper, courgette and olives and season with salt and pepper. Cover and cook on high for 3–4 hours, until all the vegetables are tender.

4. Taste and adjust the seasoning if necessary. Thinly shave the Parmesan over the top of the stew, garnish with the reserved fennel fronds and serve.

Winter Warmers

This hearty, one-pot, vegetarian dish is simplicity itself, but if you're too tired to bother with the dumplings, just serve it with fresh crusty bread.

Vegetable Hotpot with Parsley Dumplings

Ingredients

½ swede, cut into chunks

2 onions, sliced

2 potatoes, cut into chunks

2 carrots, cut into chunks

2 celery sticks, sliced

2 courgettes, sliced

2 tbsp tomato purée

600 ml/1 pint hot vegetable stock

1 bay leaf

1 tsp ground coriander

½ tsp dried thyme

salt and pepper

fresh coriander sprigs, to garnish

For the parsley dumplings

200 g/7 oz self-raising flour

115 g/4 oz vegetable suet

2 tbsp chopped fresh parsley

125 ml/4 fl oz milk

 Serves 6

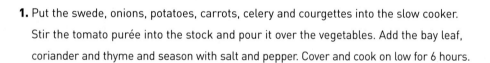 Preparation time: 20 minutes

Cooking time: 6½ hours

1. Put the swede, onions, potatoes, carrots, celery and courgettes into the slow cooker. Stir the tomato purée into the stock and pour it over the vegetables. Add the bay leaf, coriander and thyme and season with salt and pepper. Cover and cook on low for 6 hours.

2. To make the dumplings, sift the flour with a pinch of salt into a bowl and stir in the suet and parsley. Add just enough milk to make a firm but light dough. Knead lightly and shape into 12 small balls.

3. Place the dumplings on top of the stew. Cook on high for 30 minutes. Remove and discard the bay leaf and garnish with coriander sprigs. Serve immediately.

Chipotle chillies are smoked jalapeños and they impart a distinctive flavour to this dish, but remember that they are still hot.

Chipotle Chicken

Ingredients

4–6 dried chipotle chillies

4 garlic cloves, unpeeled

1 small onion, chopped

400 g/14 oz canned chopped tomatoes

300 ml/10 fl oz hot chicken or
   vegetable stock

4 skinless chicken breast portions

salt and pepper

chopped fresh flat-leaf parsley, to garnish

Serves 4

Preparation time: 10 minutes,
plus 30 minutes soaking,
plus 5–10 minutes to finish

Cooking time: 5 hours

1. Preheat the oven to 200°C/400°F/Gas Mark 6. Place the chillies in a bowl and pour in just enough hot water to cover. Set aside to soak for 30 minutes. Meanwhile, place the unpeeled garlic cloves on a baking sheet and roast in the oven for about 10 minutes until soft. Remove from the oven and set aside to cool.

2. Drain the chillies, reserving 125 ml/4 fl oz of the soaking water. Deseed the chillies, if you like, and chop coarsely. Place the chillies and reserved soaking water in a blender or food processor and process to a purée. Peel and mash the garlic in a bowl.

3. Place the chilli purée, garlic, onion and tomatoes in the slow cooker and stir in the stock. Season the chicken portions with salt and pepper and place them in the slow cooker. Cover and cook on low for about 5 hours until the chicken is tender and cooked through.

4. Lift the chicken out of the slow cooker with a slotted spoon, cover and keep warm. Pour the cooking liquid into a saucepan and bring to the boil on the hob. Boil for 5–10 minutes until reduced. Place the chicken on warmed plates, spoon the sauce over it, garnish with the chopped parsley and serve.

This makes a great vegetarian main course, but also goes well with lean roast meat, such as chicken.

Winter Vegetable Medley

Ingredients

2 tbsp sunflower oil

2 onions, peeled and chopped

3 carrots, chopped

3 parsnips, chopped

2 bunches celery, chopped, leaves reserved

2 tbsp parsley, chopped

1 tbsp fresh coriander, chopped

300 ml/10 fl oz vegetable stock

salt and pepper

 Serves 4

 Preparation time: 15 minutes, plus 10 minutes pre-cooking

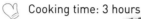 Cooking time: 3 hours

---

1. Heat the oil in a large, heavy-based saucepan. Add the onions and cook over a medium heat, stirring occasionally, for 5 minutes until softened. Add the carrots, parsnips and celery and cook, stirring occasionally, for a further 5 minutes. Stir in the herbs, season with salt and pepper and pour in the stock. Bring to the boil.

2. Transfer the vegetable mixture to the slow cooker, cover and cook on high for 3 hours until tender. Taste and adjust the seasoning if necessary. Using a slotted spoon, transfer the medley to warmed plates, then spoon over a little of the cooking liquid. Garnish with a few of the reserved celery leaves.

Hot pepper sauce is the key ingredient to the flavour of this spicy dish, but you can adjust the amount so you choose just how fiery you want it to be.

Pepper Pot-style Stew

Ingredients

1½ tbsp plain flour

450 g/1 lb stewing steak, cut into
  2.5-cm/1-inch cubes

2 tbsp olive oil

1 Spanish onion, chopped

3–4 garlic cloves, crushed

1 green chilli, deseeded and chopped

3 celery sticks, sliced

4 cloves

1 tsp ground allspice

1–2 tsp hot pepper sauce

600 ml/1 pint beef stock

225 g/8 oz peeled acorn or other squash,
  cut into small chunks

1 large red pepper, deseeded and
  chopped

4 tomatoes, coarsely chopped

115 g/4 oz okra, trimmed and halved

mixed wild and long-grain rice, to serve

Serves 4

Preparation time: 20 minutes,
plus 15 minutes pre-cooking

Cooking time: 9 hours

---

1. Spread out the flour in a shallow dish, add the steak cubes and toss until well coated. Shake off any excess and reserve the remaining flour.

2. Heat the oil in a heavy-based frying pan. Add the onion, garlic, chilli, celery, cloves and allspice and cook over a low heat, stirring occasionally, for 5 minutes until the vegetables have softened. Increase the heat to high, add the steak cubes and cook, stirring frequently, for 3 minutes until browned all over. Sprinkle in the reserved flour and cook, stirring constantly, for 2 minutes, then remove the pan from the heat.

3. Stir in the hot pepper sauce, then gradually stir in the stock. Return the pan to the heat and bring to the boil, stirring constantly. Transfer the mixture to the slow cooker and add the squash. Cover and cook on low for 8 hours.

4. Add the pepper, tomatoes and okra, re-cover and cook on high for 1 hour. Serve with mixed wild and long-grain rice

This substantial one-pot dish is terrific served on its own, with boiled rice or with crusty bread – whichever way, it will certainly keep out winter's chill.

Vegetable & Lentil Casserole

Ingredients

1 onion

10 cloves

225 g/8 oz Puy or green lentils

1 bay leaf

1.5 litres/2¾ pints vegetable stock

2 leeks, sliced

2 potatoes, diced

2 carrots, chopped

3 courgettes, sliced

1 celery stick, sliced

1 red pepper, deseeded and chopped

1 tbsp lemon juice

salt and pepper

 Serves 4

 Preparation time: 10 minutes

 Cooking time: 4½–6 hours

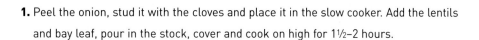

1. Peel the onion, stud it with the cloves and place it in the slow cooker. Add the lentils and bay leaf, pour in the stock, cover and cook on high for 1½–2 hours.

2. Remove the onion with a slotted spoon and re-cover the slow cooker. Remove and discard the cloves and slice the onion. Add the onion, leeks, potatoes, carrots, courgettes, celery and pepper to the lentils, season with salt and pepper, re-cover and cook on high for 3–4 hours until all the vegetables are tender.

3. Remove and discard the bay leaf and stir in the lemon juice. Taste and adjust the seasoning if necessary, then serve.

Just the aroma and appearance of this colourful dish – a fusion of European and North African cuisines – will make the family feel cosy on a freezing winter day.

Pork & Vegetable Ragout

Ingredients

450 g/1 lb lean, boneless pork

1½ tbsp plain flour

1 tsp ground coriander

1 tsp ground cumin

1½ tsp ground cinnamon

1 tbsp olive oil

1 onion, chopped

400 g/14 oz canned chopped tomatoes

2 tbsp tomato purée

300 ml/10 fl oz chicken stock

225 g/8 oz carrots, chopped

350 g/12 oz squash, such as kabocha, peeled, deseeded and chopped

225 g/8 oz leeks, sliced, blanched and drained

115 g/4 oz okra, trimmed and sliced

salt and pepper

fresh parsley sprigs, to garnish

couscous, to serve

 Serves 4

 Preparation time: 20 minutes, plus 18–20 minutes pre-cooking

 Cooking time: 5–6 hours

---

1. Trim off any visible fat from the pork and cut the flesh into thin strips about 5 cm/2 inches long. Mix together the flour, coriander, cumin and cinnamon in a shallow dish, add the pork strips and toss well to coat. Shake off the excess and reserve the remaining spiced flour.

2. Heat the oil in a heavy-based frying pan. Add the onion and cook over a low heat, stirring occasionally, for 5 minutes until softened. Add the pork strips, increase the heat to high and cook, stirring frequently, for 5 minutes until browned all over. Sprinkle in the reserved spiced flour and cook, stirring constantly, for 2 minutes, then remove the pan from the heat.

3. Gradually stir in the tomatoes with their can juices. Combine the tomato purée with the stock in a jug, then gradually stir the mixture into the frying pan. Add the carrots, return the pan to the heat and bring to the boil, stirring constantly.

4. Transfer to the slow cooker, stir in the squash, leeks and okra, and season with salt and pepper. Cover and cook on low for 5–6 hours until the meat and vegetables are tender. Garnish with parsley sprigs and serve with couscous.

Not only is this mildly spiced dish great for family meals, it is also special enough to serve to guests at an informal dinner party.

Cinnamon Lamb Casserole

Ingredients

2 tbsp plain flour

1 kg/2 lb 4 oz lean boneless lamb, cubed

2 tbsp olive oil

2 large onions, sliced

1 garlic clove, finely chopped

300 ml/10 fl oz red wine

2 tbsp red wine vinegar

400 g/14 oz canned chopped tomatoes

55 g/2 oz raisins

1 tbsp ground cinnamon

pinch of sugar

1 bay leaf

salt and pepper

To garnish

150 ml/5 fl oz Greek-style yogurt

2 garlic cloves, crushed

paprika, for sprinkling

 Serves 6

 Preparation time: 15 minutes, plus 15 minutes pre-cooking

 Cooking time: 8–8½ hours

---

1. Spread out the flour in a shallow dish and season with pepper. Add the lamb cubes and toss until well coated, shaking off any excess.

2. Heat the oil in a heavy-based frying pan. Add the onions and garlic and cook over a low heat, stirring occasionally, for 5 minutes until softened. Increase the heat to high, add the lamb and cook, stirring frequently, for 5 minutes until evenly browned.

3. Stir in the wine, vinegar and tomatoes with their can juices and bring to the boil, scraping up any sediment from the base of the pan. Transfer to the slow cooker, stir in the raisins, cinnamon, sugar and bay leaf and season with salt and pepper. Cover and cook on low for 8–8½ hours until the lamb is tender.

4. Meanwhile, prepare the garnish. Mix together the yogurt and garlic in a small bowl and season to taste with salt and pepper. Cover and chill in the refrigerator until ready to serve.

5. Remove and discard the bay leaf. Serve each portion topped with a spoonful of the garlic-flavoured yogurt sprinkled with a little paprika.

This is a wonderfully adaptable recipe that can be served with other Indian dishes or simply with plain boiled rice.

Vegetable Curry

Ingredients

2 tbsp vegetable oil

1 tsp cumin seeds

1 onion, sliced

2 curry leaves

2.5-cm/1-in piece fresh root ginger, finely chopped

2 fresh red chillies, deseeded and chopped

2 tbsp curry paste

2 carrots, sliced

115 g/4 oz mangetouts

1 cauliflower, cut into florets

3 tomatoes, peeled and chopped

85 g/3 oz frozen peas, thawed

½ tsp turmeric

150–225 ml/5–8 fl oz hot vegetable or chicken stock

salt and pepper

naan bread, to serve

Serves 4–6

Preparation time: 15 minutes, plus 20 minutes pre-cooking

Cooking time: 5 hours

1. Heat the oil in a large, heavy-based saucepan. Add the cumin seeds and cook, stirring constantly, for 1–2 minutes until they give off their aroma and begin to pop. Add the onion and curry leaves and cook, stirring occasionally, for 5 minutes until the onion has softened. Add the ginger and chillies and cook, stirring occasionally, for 1 minute.

2. Stir in the curry paste and cook, stirring, for 2 minutes, then add the carrots, mangetouts and cauliflower florets. Cook for 5 minutes, then add the tomatoes, peas and turmeric and season with salt and pepper. Cook for 3 minutes, then add 150 ml/5 fl oz of the stock and bring to the boil.

3. Transfer the mixture to the slow cooker. If the vegetables are not covered, add more hot stock, then cover and cook on low for 5 hours until tender. Remove and discard the curry leaves before serving with naan bread.

Four kinds of beans, a medley of vegetables and, of course, chillies are combined in this vibrant and delicious vegetarian main course.

Chilli Bean Stew

Ingredients

2 tbsp olive oil

1 onion, chopped

2–4 garlic cloves, chopped

2 red chillies, deseeded and chopped

225 g/8 oz drained canned red kidney
   beans, rinsed

225 g/8 oz drained canned chickpeas,
   rinsed

225 g/8 oz drained canned haricot beans,
   rinsed

1 tbsp tomato purée

700 ml/1¼ pints vegetable stock

1 red pepper, deseeded and chopped

4 tomatoes, coarsely chopped

175 g/6 oz shelled broad beans,
   thawed if frozen

1 tbsp chopped fresh coriander

soured cream, to serve

To garnish

fresh coriander sprigs

pinch of paprika

Serves 4–6

Preparation time: 15 minutes,
plus 10 minutes pre-cooking

Cooking time: 4–4½ hours

---

1. Heat the oil in a heavy-based frying pan. Add the onion, garlic and chillies and cook over a low heat, stirring occasionally, for 5 minutes until softened. Add the kidney beans, chickpeas and haricot beans. Mix together the tomato purée with a little of the stock in a jug and pour it over the beans. Add the remaining stock and bring to the boil.

2. Transfer the mixture to the slow cooker, cover and cook on low for 3 hours. Stir in the red pepper, tomatoes, broad beans and chopped coriander, re-cover and cook on high for 1–1½ hours until all the beans are tender.

3. Serve the stew topped with spoonfuls of soured cream and garnished with coriander sprigs and a sprinkling of paprika.

This colourful dish makes an economical and tasty mid-week supper when served with boiled rice.

Mixed Bean Chilli

Ingredients

2 tbsp sunflower oil

1 onion, chopped

1 garlic clove, finely chopped

1 fresh red chilli, deseeded and chopped

1 yellow pepper, deseeded and chopped

1 tsp ground cumin

1 tbsp chilli powder

115 g/4 oz dried red kidney beans, soaked overnight, drained and rinsed

115 g/4 oz dried black beans, soaked overnight, drained and rinsed

115 g/4 oz dried pinto beans, soaked overnight, drained and rinsed

1 litre/1¾ pints vegetable stock

1 tbsp sugar

salt and pepper

chopped fresh coriander, to garnish

 Serves 4–6

 Preparation time: 10 minutes, plus overnight soaking, plus 25 minutes pre-cooking

 Cooking time: 10 hours

---

1. Heat the oil in a large, heavy-based saucepan. Add the onion, garlic, chilli and yellow pepper and cook over a medium heat, stirring occasionally, for 5 minutes. Stir in the cumin and chilli powder and cook, stirring, for 1–2 minutes. Add the drained beans and stock and bring to the boil. Boil vigorously for 15 minutes.

2. Transfer the mixture to the slow cooker, cover and cook on low for 10 hours until the beans are tender.

3. Season the mixture with salt and pepper, then ladle about one-third into a bowl. Mash well with a potato masher, then return the mashed beans to the cooker and stir in the sugar. Serve immediately, sprinkled with chopped fresh coriander.

Cook's tip

Both kidney beans and black beans contain a toxin (pinto beans don't) that is destroyed by vigorous boiling. It is important, therefore, that they are pre-cooked before being transferred to the slow cooker.

This is an inexpensive and easy version of a much more elaborate and time-consuming French dish – but it's very good on a cold evening.

Poor Man's Cassoulet

Ingredients

2 tbsp sunflower oil

2 onions, chopped

2 garlic cloves, finely chopped

115 g/4 oz streaky bacon, derinded and chopped

500 g/1 lb 2 oz pork sausages

400 g/14 oz canned haricot, red kidney or black-eyed beans, drained and rinsed

2 tbsp chopped fresh parsley

150 ml/5 fl oz hot beef stock

To serve

4 slices French bread

55 g/2 oz Gruyère cheese, grated

 Serves 4

 Preparation time: 10 minutes, plus 10 minutes pre-cooking

Cooking time: 6 hours

---

1. Heat the oil in a heavy-based frying pan. Add the onions and cook over a low heat, stirring occasionally, for 5 minutes until softened. Add the garlic, bacon and sausages and cook, stirring and turning the sausages occasionally, for a further 5 minutes.

2. Using a slotted spoon, transfer the mixture from the frying pan to the slow cooker. Add the beans, parsley and beef stock, then cover and cook on low for 6 hours.

3. Just before serving, lightly toast the bread under a preheated grill. Divide the grated cheese among the toast slices and place under the grill until just melted.

4. Ladle the stew onto warmed plates, top each portion with the cheese-toast and serve.

While this is certainly not a traditional recipe, this vegetarian version is filling, nourishing and packed with flavour.

Vegetable Goulash

Ingredients

15 g/½ oz sun-dried tomatoes, chopped

2 tbsp olive oil

½–1 tsp crushed dried chillies

2–3 garlic cloves, chopped

1 large onion, cut into small wedges

1 small celeriac, cut into small chunks

225 g/8 oz carrots, sliced

225 g/8 oz new potatoes, cut into chunks

1 small acorn squash, peeled, deseeded
   and chopped

2 tbsp tomato purée

300 ml/10 fl oz vegetable stock

225 g/8 oz Puy lentils

1–2 tsp hot paprika

3 fresh thyme sprigs, plus extra to garnish

450 g/1 lb tomatoes

soured cream, to serve

 Serves 4

 Preparation time: 20 minutes,
   plus 15–20 minutes soaking,
   plus 10–12 minutes pre-cooking

 Cooking time: 5¼ hours

1. Put the sun-dried tomatoes in a small heatproof bowl, add freshly boiled water to cover and leave to soak for 15–20 minutes.

2. Heat the oil in a heavy-based saucepan. Add the chillies, garlic, onion, celeriac, carrots, potatoes and squash and cook over a medium–low heat, stirring frequently, for 5–8 minutes until softened. Mix together the tomato purée and stock in a jug and stir it into the pan. Add the lentils, sun-dried tomatoes with their soaking liquid, the paprika and thyme and bring to the boil.

3. Transfer the mixture to the slow cooker, cover and cook on low for 4½ hours. Add the tomatoes, re-cover and cook on high for 45 minutes until all the vegetables and lentils are tender. Remove and discard the thyme sprigs. Serve the goulash topped with soured cream and garnished with extra thyme sprigs.

This is a great dish to serve at an informal dinner party, with plenty of salad and fresh crusty bread for mopping up the tasty juices.

Duckling Jambalaya-style Stew

Ingredients

4 duckling breasts, about 175 g/6 oz each

2 tbsp olive oil

225 g/8 oz gammon, cut into small chunks

225 g/8 oz chorizo or other spicy
   sausages, skinned and sliced

1 onion, chopped

3 garlic cloves, chopped

3 celery sticks, chopped

1–2 red chillies, deseeded and chopped

1 green pepper, deseeded and chopped

600 ml/1 pint chicken stock

1 tbsp chopped fresh oregano

400 g/14 oz canned chopped tomatoes

1–2 tsp hot pepper sauce

fresh parsley sprigs, to garnish

To serve

green salad

boiled rice

 Serves 4

 Preparation time: 15 minutes,
   plus 12–15 minutes pre-cooking

 Cooking time: 6 hours

---

1. Remove and discard the skin and any visible fat from the duckling breasts and cut the flesh into bite-size pieces. Heat half the oil in a heavy-based frying pan, add the duckling, gammon and chorizo and cook over a high heat, stirring frequently, for 5 minutes until browned all over. Using a slotted spoon, transfer the meat to the slow cooker.

2. Add the onion, garlic, celery and chilli to the frying pan, lower the heat and cook, stirring occasionally, for 5 minutes until softened. Add the green pepper and stir in the stock, oregano, tomatoes with the can juices and hot pepper sauce. Bring to the boil, then pour the mixture over the meat.

3. Cover the slow cooker and cook on low for 6 hours, until the meat is tender. Serve garnished with parsley sprigs and accompanied by a green salad and boiled rice.

This is a great dish for informal entertaining as long as your guests don't mind its being slightly messy to eat. Finger bowls are essential.

Shellfish Stew

Ingredients

1 tbsp olive oil

115 g/4 oz bacon, diced

2 tbsp butter

2 shallots, chopped

2 leeks, sliced

2 celery sticks, chopped

2 potatoes, diced

675 g/1 lb 8 oz tomatoes, peeled,
     deseeded and chopped

3 tbsp chopped fresh parsley

3 tbsp snipped fresh chives,
     plus extra to garnish

1 bay leaf

1 fresh thyme sprig

1.4 litres/2½ pints fish stock

24 live mussels

24 live clams

450 g/1 lb sea bream fillets

24 raw tiger prawns

salt and pepper

 Serves 8

 Preparation time: 20 minutes,
     plus 20 minutes pre-cooking

 Cooking time: 7½ hours

---

1. Heat the oil in a heavy-based frying pan. Add the bacon and cook, stirring frequently, for 5–8 minutes until crisp. Using a slotted spoon, transfer to the slow cooker. Add the butter to the frying pan and when it has melted, add the shallots, leeks, celery and potatoes. Cook over a low heat, stirring occasionally, for 5 minutes until softened. Stir in the tomatoes, parsley, chives, bay leaf and thyme, pour in the stock and bring to the boil, stirring constantly. Pour the mixture into the slow cooker, cover and cook on low for 7 hours.

2. Meanwhile, scrub the mussels and clams under cold running water and pull off the 'beards' from the mussels. Discard any with broken shells or that do not shut immediately when sharply tapped. Cut the fish fillets into bite-size chunks. Peel and devein the prawns.

3. Remove and discard the bay leaf and thyme sprig from the stew. Season with salt and pepper and add all the fish and seafood. Re-cover and cook on high for 30 minutes. Serve garnished with extra chives.

Around the World

This dish has been an American favourite for almost as long as the United States has existed and shows how New World ingredients gave new vitality to Old World cooking.

Brunswick Stew

Ingredients

1.8 kg/4 lb chicken portions

2 tbsp paprika

2 tbsp olive oil

2 tbsp butter

450 g/1 lb onions, chopped

2 yellow peppers, deseeded and chopped

400 g/14 oz canned chopped tomatoes

225 ml/8 fl oz dry white wine

450 ml/16 fl oz chicken stock

1 tbsp Worcestershire sauce

½ tsp Tabasco sauce

1 tbsp finely chopped fresh parsley

2 tbsp plain flour

325 g/11½ oz canned sweetcorn kernels, drained

425 g/15 oz canned butter beans, drained and rinsed

salt

fresh parsley sprigs, to garnish

 Serves 6

Preparation time: 15 minutes, plus 20 minutes pre-cooking

Cooking time: 5½ hours

---

1. Season the chicken portions with salt and dust with the paprika. Heat the oil and butter in a heavy-based frying pan. Add the chicken portions and cook over a medium–high heat, turning frequently, for 10 minutes until golden brown all over. Using a slotted spoon, transfer the chicken to the slow cooker.

2. Add the onions and peppers to the frying pan, lower the heat and cook, stirring occasionally, for 5 minutes until softened. Add the tomatoes with their can juices, wine, stock, Worcestershire sauce, Tabasco sauce and chopped parsley and bring to the boil, stirring constantly. Pour the mixture over the chicken, cover and cook on low for 5 hours.

3. Mix the flour with 4 tbsp water to a paste in a small, heatproof bowl. Add a ladleful of the cooking liquid and mix well, then stir the mixture into the stew. Add the sweetcorn and butter beans, re-cover and cook on high for 30 minutes until the chicken is tender and cooked through. Serve garnished with parsley sprigs.

Pork is traditionally served with sharp-flavoured fruit to counterbalance its richness. This unusual and refreshing recipe uses pineapple to do this.

Mexican Pork Chops

Ingredients

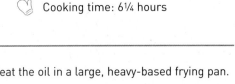

4 pork chops, trimmed of excess fat

2 tbsp sunflower oil

450 g/1 lb canned pineapple cubes in
   fruit juice

1 red pepper, deseeded and finely chopped

2 fresh jalapeño chillies, deseeded and
   finely chopped

1 onion, finely chopped

1 tbsp chopped fresh coriander

125 ml/4 fl oz hot chicken stock

salt and pepper

fresh coriander sprigs, to garnish

tortillas, to serve

Serves 4

Preparation time: 15 minutes,
plus 10 minutes pre-cooking

Cooking time: 6¼ hours

---

1. Season the chops with salt and pepper. Heat the oil in a large, heavy-based frying pan. Add the chops and cook over a medium heat for 2–3 minutes each side until lightly browned. Transfer them to the slow cooker. Drain the pineapple, reserving the juice, and set aside.

2. Add the red pepper, chillies and onion to the frying pan and cook, stirring occasionally, for 5 minutes until the onion is softened. Transfer the mixture to the slow cooker and add the coriander and stock, together with 125 ml/4 fl oz of the reserved pineapple juice. Cover and cook on low for 6 hours until the chops are tender.

3. Add the reserved pineapple to the slow cooker, re-cover and cook on high for 15 minutes. Garnish with fresh coriander sprigs and serve immediately, with tortillas.

This summery dish from the Sunshine State is sure to bring a smile to the faces of your guests or family whatever time of year you serve it.

Florida Chicken

Ingredients

1½ tbsp plain flour

450 g/1 lb skinless, boneless chicken,
   cut into bite-size pieces

1 tbsp olive oil

1 onion, cut into wedges

2 celery sticks, sliced

150 ml/5 fl oz orange juice

300 ml/10 fl oz chicken stock

1 tbsp light soy sauce

1–2 tsp clear honey

1 tbsp grated orange rind

1 orange pepper, deseeded and chopped

225 g/8 oz courgettes, halved lengthways
   and sliced

2 corn on the cobs

1 orange, peeled and segmented

salt and pepper

1 tbsp chopped fresh parsley, to garnish

 Serves 4

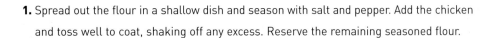 Preparation time: 15 minutes,
   plus 15 minutes pre-cooking

 Cooking time: 5¼ hours

---

1. Spread out the flour in a shallow dish and season with salt and pepper. Add the chicken and toss well to coat, shaking off any excess. Reserve the remaining seasoned flour.

2. Heat the oil in a heavy-based frying pan. Add the chicken and cook over a high heat, stirring frequently, for 5 minutes until golden brown all over. Using a slotted spoon, transfer the chicken to the slow cooker.

3. Add the onion and celery to the frying pan, lower the heat and cook, stirring occasionally, for 5 minutes until softened. Sprinkle in the reserved seasoned flour and cook, stirring constantly, for 2 minutes. Remove the pan from the heat. Gradually stir in the orange juice, stock, soy sauce and honey, then add the orange rind. Return the pan to the heat and bring to the boil, stirring constantly.

4. Pour the mixture over the chicken and add the pepper, courgettes and corn on the cobs. Cover and cook on low for 5 hours until the chicken is tender and cooked through. Stir in the orange segments, re-cover and cook on high for 15 minutes. Serve garnished with the parsley.

Packed with flavour and bursting with colour, this is a perfect dish to come home to after a busy day.

Caribbean Beef Stew

Ingredients

450 g/1 lb braising steak

450 g/1 lb diced pumpkin or other squash

1 onion, chopped

1 red pepper, deseeded and chopped

2 garlic cloves, finely chopped

2.5-cm/1-inch piece fresh root ginger, finely chopped

1 tbsp sweet or hot paprika

225 ml/8 fl oz beef stock

400 g/14 oz canned chopped tomatoes

400g/14 oz canned pigeon peas, drained and rinsed

400 g/14 oz canned black-eyed beans, drained and rinsed

salt and pepper

 Serves 6

Preparation time: 20 minutes, plus 10 minutes pre-cooking

Cooking time: 7½ hours

1. Trim off any visible fat from the steak, then dice the meat. Heat a large, heavy-based saucepan without adding any extra fat. Add the meat and cook, stirring constantly, for a few minutes until golden all over. Stir in the pumpkin, onion and red pepper and cook for 1 minute, then add the ginger, paprika stock and tomatoes and bring to the boil.

2. Transfer the mixture to the slow cooker, cover and cook on low for 7 hours. Add the pigeon peas and black-eyed beans to the stew and season to taste with salt and pepper. Re-cover and cook on high for 30 minutes, then serve.

This Louisiana classic is thought to get its name from the French jambon or the Spanish jamón – meaning ham, which is a traditional ingredient.

Jambalaya

Ingredients

½ tsp cayenne pepper

½ tsp freshly ground black pepper

1 tsp salt

2 tsp chopped fresh thyme

350 g/12 oz skinless, boneless chicken breasts, diced

2 tbsp sunflower oil

2 onions, chopped

2 garlic cloves, finely chopped

2 green peppers, deseeded and chopped

2 celery sticks, chopped

115 g/4 oz smoked ham, chopped

175 g/6 oz chorizo sausage, sliced

400 g/14 oz canned chopped tomatoes

2 tbsp tomato purée

225 ml/8 fl oz chicken stock

450 g/1 lb peeled raw prawns

450 g/1 lb cooked rice

snipped fresh chives, to garnish

 Serves 6

 Preparation time: 20 minutes, plus 15 minutes pre-cooking

 Cooking time: 6½ hours

---

1. Mix together the cayenne, black pepper, salt and thyme in a bowl. Add the chicken and toss to coat. Heat the oil in a large, heavy-based saucepan. Add the onions, garlic, green peppers and celery and cook over a low heat, stirring occasionally, for 5 minutes. Add the chicken and cook over a medium heat, stirring frequently, for a further 5 minutes until golden all over. Stir in the ham, chorizo, tomatoes, tomato purée and stock and bring to the boil.

2. Transfer the mixture to the slow cooker. Cover and cook on low for 6 hours. Add the prawns and rice, re-cover and cook on high for 30 minutes.

3. Taste and adjust the seasoning, if necessary. Transfer to warm plates, garnish with chives and serve the jambalaya immediately.

It is well worth buying a full-bodied, good-quality red wine-preferably Burgundy - for this perennially popular French classic.

Boeuf Bourguignonne

Ingredients

6 rashers streaky bacon, derinded and chopped

2 tbsp plain flour

900 g/2 lb braising steak, trimmed and cut into 2.5-cm/1-inch cubes

3 tbsp olive oil

25 g/1 oz unsalted butter

12 baby onions or shallots

2 garlic cloves, finely chopped

150 ml/5 fl oz beef stock

450 ml/16 fl oz full-bodied red wine

bouquet garni

140 g/5 oz mushrooms, sliced

salt and pepper

 Serves 6

 Preparation time: 15 minutes, plus 15 minutes pre-cooking

Cooking time: 7¼ hours

---

1. Cook the bacon in a large, heavy-based saucepan, stirring occasionally, until the fat runs and the pieces are crisp. Meanwhile, spread out the flour on a plate and season with salt and pepper. Toss the steak cubes in the flour to coat, shaking off any excess. Using a slotted spoon, transfer the bacon to a plate. Add the oil to the saucepan. When it is hot, add the steak cubes and cook, in batches, stirring occasionally, for 5 minutes until browned all over. Transfer to the plate with a slotted spoon.

2. Add the butter to the saucepan. When it has melted, add the onions and garlic and cook, stirring occasionally, for 5 minutes. Return the bacon and steak to the pan and pour in the stock and wine. Bring to the boil.

3. Transfer the mixture to the slow cooker and add the bouquet garni. Cover and cook on low for 7 hours until the meat is tender.

4. Add the mushrooms to the slow cooker and stir well. Re-cover and cook on high for 15 minutes.

5. Remove and discard the bouquet garni. Adjust the seasoning if necessary, then serve immediately.

All French coastal regions have their own speciality fish stew. Packed with the flavours of the Mediterranean, this is undoubtedly one of the most delicious.

French-style Fish Stew

Ingredients

large pinch of saffron threads
900 g/2 lb mixed white fish, such as
    sea bass, monkfish, red mullet and
    grouper, filleted
24 large raw prawns
1 prepared squid
2 tbsp olive oil
1 large onion, finely chopped
1 fennel bulb, thinly sliced, feathery
    fronds reserved
2 large garlic cloves, crushed
4 tbsp Pernod
1 litre/1¾ pints fish stock

2 large tomatoes, peeled, deseeded and
    diced, or 400 g/14 oz canned chopped
    tomatoes, drained
1 tbsp tomato purée
1 bay leaf
pinch of sugar
pinch of dried chilli flakes (optional)
salt and pepper

 Serves 4–6

Preparation time: 25 minutes,
plus 10–12 minutes pre-cooking

Cooking time: 6½ hours

---

1. Toast the saffron threads in a small, dry frying pan over a high heat, stirring constantly for 1 minute until they give off their aroma. Tip into a bowl and set aside. Cut the fish fillets into large chunks. Peel and devein the prawns, reserving the heads and shells. Cut off and reserve the tentacles from the squid and slice the body into 5-mm/¼-inch rings. Place the seafood in a bowl, cover and chill in the refrigerator until required. Tie the heads and shells of the prawns in a piece of muslin.

2. Heat the oil in a heavy-based frying pan. Add the onion and fennel and cook over a low heat, stirring occasionally, for 5 minutes until softened. Add the garlic and cook, stirring frequently, for 2 minutes. Remove the pan from the heat. Heat the Pernod in a ladle or small saucepan, ignite and pour it over the onion and fennel, gently shaking the frying pan until the flames have died down.

3. Return the frying pan to the heat, stir in the toasted saffron, stock, tomatoes, tomato purée, bay leaf, sugar and chilli flakes, if using, and season with salt and pepper. Bring to the boil, then transfer to the slow cooker, add the bag of prawn shells, cover and cook on low for 6 hours.

4. Remove and discard the bag of prawn shells and the bay leaf. Add the fish and seafood to the slow cooker, cover and cook on high for 30 minutes until the fish flakes easily with the point of a knife. Serve garnished with the reserved fennel fronds.

This is only one, although perhaps the most famous, of Mediterranean fish soups. For the best flavour, it should include a variety of different fish.

Bouillabaisse

Ingredients

2.25 kg/5 lb mixed white fish, such as red mullet, sea bream, sea bass, monkfish and whiting, filleted and bones and heads reserved, if possible
450 g/1 lb raw prawns
grated rind of 1 orange
pinch of saffron threads
4 garlic cloves, finely chopped
225 ml/8 fl oz olive oil
2 onions, finely chopped
1 leek, thinly sliced
4 potatoes, thinly sliced
2 large tomatoes, peeled and chopped

1 bunch fresh flat-leaf parsley, chopped
1 fresh fennel sprig
1 fresh thyme sprig
1 bay leaf
2 cloves
6 black peppercorns
1 strip orange rind
sea salt
crusty bread or croûtes, to serve

 Serves 6

 Preparation time: 45 minutes

 Cooking time: 8½ hours

1. Cut the fish fillets into bite-sized pieces and peel and devein the prawns. Reserve the heads and shells of the prawns. Rinse the fish bones, if using, and cut off the gills of any fish heads. Place the chunks of fish and the prawns in a large bowl. Sprinkle with the grated orange rind, saffron, half the garlic and 2 tablespoons of the oil. Cover and set aside in the refrigerator.

2. Put the remaining garlic, the onions, leek, potatoes, tomatoes, parsley, fennel, thyme, bay leaf, cloves, peppercorns and strip of orange rind in the slow cooker. Add the fish heads and bones, if using, and the prawn shells and heads. Pour in the remaining olive oil and 2.8 litres/5 pints boiling water or enough to cover the ingredients by 2.5 cm/1 inch. Season with sea salt. Cover and cook on low for 8 hours.

3. Strain the stock and return the liquid to the slow cooker. Discard the flavourings, fish and prawn trimmings but retain the vegetables and return them to the slow cooker if you like. Add the fish and prawn mixture, re-cover and cook on high for 30 minutes until the fish is cooked through and flakes easily with the point of a knife.

4. Ladle into warm bowls and serve with crusty bread or croûtes.

This fabulous combination of sweet and savoury, refreshing and warming flavours is typical of the Maghreb – the area of North Africa that includes Algeria, Morocco and Tunisia.

Mediterranean Lamb with Apricots & Pistachio Nuts

Ingredients

pinch of saffron threads

450 g/1 lb boneless lamb leg steaks

1½ tbsp plain flour

1 tsp ground coriander

½ tsp ground cumin

½ tsp ground allspice

1 tbsp olive oil

1 onion, chopped

2–3 garlic cloves, chopped

450 ml/16 fl oz lamb or chicken stock

1 cinnamon stick

85 g/3 oz dried apricots, chopped

175 g/6 oz courgettes, sliced

115 g/4 oz cherry tomatoes

1 tbsp chopped fresh coriander

salt and pepper

2 tbsp coarsely chopped pistachio nuts, to garnish

couscous or rice, to serve

 Serves 4

 Preparation time: 20 minutes, plus 15 minutes pre-cooking

 Cooking time: 8 hours

---

1. Put the saffron threads in a small heatproof bowl, add 2 tbsp freshly boiled water and leave to infuse for 10 minutes. Meanwhile, trim off any visible fat from the lamb steaks and cut the flesh into 2.5-cm/1-inch chunks. Mix together the flour, ground coriander, cumin and allspice in a shallow dish, add the lamb and toss until well coated, shaking off any excess. Reserve the remaining spiced flour.

2. Heat the oil in a heavy-based frying pan. Add the onion and garlic and cook over a low heat, stirring occasionally, for 5 minutes until softened. Add the pieces of lamb, increase the heat to high and cook, stirring frequently, for 3 minutes until browned on all sides. Sprinkle in the reserved spiced flour and cook, stirring constantly, for 2 minutes, then remove the pan from the heat.

3. Gradually stir in the stock and the saffron with its soaking liquid. Return the pan to the heat and bring to the boil, stirring constantly. Transfer the mixture to the slow cooker and add the cinnamon stick, apricots, courgettes and tomatoes. Cover and cook on low for 8 hours until the meat is tender.

4. Remove and discard the cinnamon stick. Stir in the chopped coriander, season to taste with salt and pepper, sprinkle with the pistachio nuts and serve with couscous or rice.

This colourful vegetarian sauce is a little like the classic French dish ratatouille but has an extra tang of balsamic vinegar and lemon juice.

Sweet-and-Sour Sicilian Pasta

Ingredients

4 tbsp olive oil

1 large red onion, sliced

2 garlic cloves, finely chopped

2 red peppers, deseeded and sliced

2 courgettes, cut into batons

1 aubergine, cut into batons

450 ml/16 fl oz passata

4 tbsp lemon juice

2 tbsp balsamic vinegar

55 g/2 oz stoned black olives, sliced

1 tbsp sugar

400 g/14 oz dried fettucine or pappardelle

salt and pepper

fresh flat-leaf parsley sprigs, to garnish

 Serves 4

 Preparation time: 15 minutes, plus 15 minutes pre-cooking

 Cooking time: 5 hours

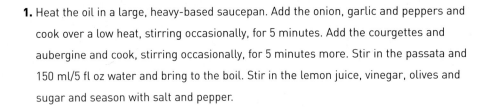

1. Heat the oil in a large, heavy-based saucepan. Add the onion, garlic and peppers and cook over a low heat, stirring occasionally, for 5 minutes. Add the courgettes and aubergine and cook, stirring occasionally, for 5 minutes more. Stir in the passata and 150 ml/5 fl oz water and bring to the boil. Stir in the lemon juice, vinegar, olives and sugar and season with salt and pepper.

2. Transfer the mixture to the slow cooker. Cover and cook on low for 5 hours until all the vegetables are tender.

3. To cook the pasta, bring a large saucepan of lightly salted water to the boil. Add the pasta and bring back to the boil. Cook for 10–12 minutes until the pasta is tender but still firm to the bite. Drain and transfer to a warmed serving dish. Spoon the vegetable mixture over the pasta, toss lightly, garnish with parsley and serve.

This is a classically simple dish that relies on using the best-quality ingredients in a complementary combination, all delicately flavoured with thyme.

Chicken Italian-style

Ingredients

1 tbsp plain flour

4 chicken portions, about 175 g/6 oz each

2½ tbsp olive oil

8–12 shallots, halved if large

2–4 garlic cloves, sliced

400 ml/14 fl oz chicken stock

50 ml/2 fl oz dry sherry

4 fresh thyme sprigs

115 g/4 oz cherry tomatoes

115 g/4 oz baby sweetcorn, halved lengthways

2 slices white or wholemeal bread, crusts removed

salt and pepper

1 tbsp chopped fresh thyme, to garnish

 Serves 4

Preparation time: 10 minutes, plus 20 minutes pre-cooking

Cooking time: 5–6 hours

---

1. Spread out the flour in a shallow dish and season with salt and pepper. Add the chicken portions and toss well to coat, shaking off any excess. Reserve the remaining seasoned flour.

2. Heat 1 tbsp of the oil in a heavy-based frying pan. Add the chicken portions and cook over a medium–high heat, turning frequently, for 10 minutes until golden brown all over. Using a slotted spoon, transfer the chicken to the slow cooker.

3. Add the shallots and garlic to the frying pan, lower the heat and cook, stirring occasionally, for 5 minutes until softened. Sprinkle in the reserved seasoned flour and cook, stirring constantly, for 2 minutes. Remove the pan from the heat and gradually stir in the stock and sherry. Return the pan to the heat and bring to the boil, stirring constantly.

4. Pour the mixture over the chicken and add the thyme sprigs, tomatoes and baby sweetcorn. Cover and cook on low for 5–6 hours until the chicken is tender and cooked through.

5. Meanwhile, cut the bread into cubes. Heat the remaining oil in a frying pan, add the bread cubes and cook, stirring frequently, for 4–5 minutes until golden all over. Remove and discard the thyme sprigs from the stew, then serve, garnished with the croûtons and chopped thyme.

Most regions of Italy boast of their stufato – slow-braised beef – and, hardly surprisingly, in Naples the recipe includes tomatoes.

Neapolitan Beef

Ingredients

300 ml/10 fl oz red wine

4 tbsp olive oil

1 celery stick, chopped

2 shallots, sliced

4 garlic cloves, finely chopped

1 bay leaf

10 fresh basil leaves, plus extra to garnish

3 fresh parsley sprigs

pinch of grated nutmeg

pinch of ground cinnamon

2 cloves

1.5 kg/3 lb 5 oz beef silverside

1–2 garlic cloves, thinly sliced

55 g/2 oz streaky bacon or pancetta, derinded and chopped

400g/14 oz canned chopped tomatoes

2 tbsp tomato purée

 Serves 6

 Preparation time: 15 minutes, plus 12 hours marinating plus 15 minutes pre-cooking

 Cooking time: 9 hours

---

1. Combine the wine, 2 tablespoons of the olive oil, the celery, shallots, garlic, herbs and spices in a large, non-metallic bowl. Add the beef, cover and marinate, turning occasionally, for 12 hours.

2. Drain the beef, reserving the marinade, and pat dry with kitchen paper. Make small incisions all over the beef using a sharp knife. Insert a slice of garlic and a piece of bacon in each 'pocket'. Heat the remaining oil in a large frying pan. Add the meat and cook over a medium heat, turning frequently, until browned all over. Transfer to the slow cooker.

3. Strain the reserved marinade into the frying pan and bring to the boil. Stir in the tomatoes and tomato purée. Stir well, then pour the mixture over the beef. Cover and cook on low for about 9 hours until tender. If possible, turn the beef over halfway through the cooking time. To serve, remove the beef and place on a carving board. Cover with foil and leave to stand for 10–15 minutes to firm up. Cut into slices and transfer to a platter. Spoon over the sauce, garnish with basil and serve immediately.

Delicate North African spices complement the delicious flavour of this attractive fish, which is usually cooked whole.

Moroccan Sea Bream

Ingredients

2 tbsp olive oil

2 onions, chopped

2 garlic cloves, finely chopped

2 carrots, finely chopped

1 fennel bulb, finely chopped

½ tsp ground cumin

½ tsp ground cloves

1 tsp ground coriander

pinch of saffron threads

300 ml/10 fl oz fish stock

1 preserved or fresh lemon

900 g/2 lb sea bream, cleaned

salt and pepper

 Serves 2

 Preparation time: 15 minutes, plus 10 minutes pre-cooking, plus 5 minutes to finish

 Cooking time: 6½–6¾ hours

1. Heat the oil in a large, heavy-based saucepan. Add the onions, garlic, carrots and fennel and cook over a medium heat, stirring occasionally, for 5 minutes. Stir in all the spices and cook, stirring, for a further 2 minutes. Pour in the stock, season with salt and pepper and bring to the boil.

2. Transfer the mixture to the slow cooker. Cover and cook on low for 6 hours or until the vegetables are tender.

3. Rinse the preserved lemon if using. Discard the fish head if you like. Slice the lemon and place the slices in the fish cavity, then place the fish in the slow cooker. Re-cover and cook on high for 30–45 minutes until the flesh flakes easily with the point of a knife.

4. Carefully transfer the fish to a platter and spoon the vegetables around it. Cover and keep warm. Transfer the cooking liquid to a saucepan and boil for a few minutes until reduced. Spoon it over the fish and serve.

This is a great main course dish for vegetarians and can also be served as an accompaniment to roast lamb or baked fish.

Moroccan Vegetable Stew

Ingredients

4 tomatoes, peeled, deseeded and chopped

700 ml/1¼ pints vegetable stock

1 onion, sliced

2 carrots, diagonally sliced

1 tbsp chopped fresh coriander

175 g/6 oz courgettes, sliced

1 small turnip, cubed

425 g/15 oz canned chickpeas, drained and rinsed

½ tsp ground turmeric

¼ tsp ground ginger

¼ tsp ground cinnamon

225 g/8 oz couscous

salt

fresh coriander sprigs, to garnish

 Serves 4

 Preparation time: 15 minutes, plus 10 minutes pre-cooking

 Cooking time: 3 hours

---

1. Put half the tomatoes in a blender or food processor and process until smooth. Scrape into a saucepan, add 450 ml/16 fl oz of the stock and bring to the boil. Pour the mixture into the slow cooker, add the remaining tomatoes, the onion, carrots, coriander, courgettes, turnip, chickpeas, turmeric, ginger and cinnamon and stir well. Cover and cook on high for 3 hours.

2. Just before serving, bring the remaining stock to the boil in a large pan. Add a pinch of salt and sprinkle in the couscous, stirring constantly. Remove the pan from the heat, cover and leave to stand for 5 minutes.

3. Fluff up the grains of couscous with a fork and divide it among 4 bowls. Top with the vegetable stew, garnish with coriander sprigs and serve.

East meets West in Bulgarian cuisine, as typified by the combination of sweet paprika and hot chilli in this classic dish.

Bulgarian Chicken

Ingredients

4 tbsp sunflower oil

6 chicken portions

2 onions, chopped

2 garlic cloves, finely chopped

1 fresh red chilli, deseeded and
   finely chopped

6 tomatoes, peeled and chopped

2 tsp sweet paprika

1 bay leaf

225 ml/8 fl oz hot chicken stock

salt and pepper

 Serves 6

 Preparation time: 20 minutes,
   plus 10 minutes pre-cooking

 Cooking time: 6 hours

1. Heat the oil in a large, heavy-based frying pan. Add the chicken portions and cook over a medium heat, turning occasionally, for about 10 minutes, until golden all over.

2. Transfer the contents of the pan to the slow cooker and add the onions, garlic, chilli and tomatoes. Sprinkle in the paprika, add the bay leaf and pour in the stock. Season with salt and pepper. Stir well, cover and cook on low for 6 hours until the chicken is cooked through and tender. Remove and discard the bay leaf, then serve immediately.

This is simplicity itself, requiring very little preparation, yet it is packed with flavour and makes a great midweek supper. Serve with rice for a more substantial dish.

Easy Chinese Chicken

Ingredients

2 tsp grated fresh root ginger

4 garlic cloves, finely chopped

2 star anise

150 ml/5 fl oz Chinese rice wine or
    medium dry sherry

2 tbsp dark soy sauce

1 tsp sesame oil

4 skinless chicken thighs or drumsticks

shredded spring onions, to garnish

 Serves 4

 Preparation time: 10 minutes,
plus 5 minutes pre-cooking

 Cooking time: 4 hours

---

1. Mix together the ginger, garlic, star anise, rice wine, soy sauce and sesame oil in a bowl and stir in 5 tablespoons of water. Place the chicken in a saucepan, add the spice mixture and bring to the boil.

2. Transfer to the slow cooker, cover and cook on low for 4 hours or until the chicken is tender and cooked through.

3. Remove and discard the star anise. Transfer the chicken to warmed plates and serve garnished with shredded spring onions.

Contrasting flavours, colours and textures make this tasty and attractive dish a perennial favourite among adults and children alike.

Pork Oriental

Ingredients

450 g/1 lb lean boneless pork

1½ tbsp plain flour

1–2 tbsp groundnut oil

1 onion, cut into small wedges

2–3 garlic cloves, chopped

2.5-cm/1-inch piece fresh root ginger, grated

1 red pepper, deseeded and sliced

1 green pepper, deseeded and sliced

1 tbsp tomato purée

300 ml/10 fl oz chicken stock

225 g/8 oz canned pineapple chunks in
   natural juice

1–1½ tbsp dark soy sauce

1½ tbsp rice vinegar

4 spring onions, diagonally sliced, to garnish

rice, to serve

 Serves 4

 Preparation time: 15 minutes,
plus 15 minutes pre-cooking

 Cooking time: 5½–6½ hours

---

1. Trim off all visible fat from the pork and cut the flesh into 2.5-cm/1-inch chunks. Spread out the flour in a shallow dish, add the pork and toss well to coat, shaking off any excess. Reserve the remaining flour.

2. Heat the oil in a heavy-based frying pan. Add the onion, garlic, ginger and peppers and cook over a low heat, stirring occasionally, for 5 minutes until softened. Add the pork, increase the heat and cook, stirring frequently, for 5 minutes until browned all over. Sprinkle in the reserved flour and cook, stirring constantly, for 2 minutes, then remove the pan from the heat.

3. Mix the tomato purée and stock in a jug, then gradually stir into the frying pan. Drain the pineapple, reserving the juice. Stir the juice and soy sauce into the pan. Return the pan to the heat and bring to the boil, stirring constantly. Transfer to the slow cooker, cover and cook on low for 5–6 hours.

4. Stir in the pineapple and vinegar, re-cover and cook on high for 30 minutes. Garnish with the sliced spring onions and serve with rice.

Desserts

This deliciously tangy dessert is a good, old-fashioned family favourite that looks and smells tempting and tastes scrumptious.

Magic Lemon Sponge

Ingredients

140 g/5 oz caster sugar

3 eggs, separated

300 ml/10 fl oz milk

3 tbsp self-raising flour, sifted

150 ml/5 fl oz freshly squeezed lemon juice

icing sugar, for dusting

Serves 4

Preparation time: 20 minutes

Cooking time: 2½ hours

---

1. Beat the sugar with the egg yolks in a bowl, using an electric mixer. Gradually beat in the milk, followed by the flour and the lemon juice.

2. Whisk the egg whites in a separate, grease-free bowl until stiff. Fold half the whites into the yolk mixture using a rubber or plastic spatula in a figure-of-eight movement, then fold in the remainder. Try not to knock out the air.

3. Pour the mixture into an ovenproof dish, cover with foil and place in the slow cooker. Add sufficient boiling water to come about one-third of the way up the side of the dish. Cover and cook on high for 2½ hours until the mixture has set and the sauce and sponge have separated.

4. Lift the dish out of the cooker and discard the foil. Lightly sift a little icing sugar over the top and serve.

Served hot or cold, on its own or accompanied by cream, custard or ice cream, this is always a sure-fire family favourite.

Apple Crumble

Ingredients

55 g/2 oz plain flour

55 g/2 oz rolled oats

150 g/5½ oz light muscovado sugar

½ tsp grated nutmeg

½ tsp ground cinnamon

115 g/4 oz butter, softened

4 cooking apples, peeled, cored and sliced

4–5 tbsp apple juice

single cream or natural yogurt, to serve

Serves 4

Preparation time: 15 minutes

Cooking time: 5½ hours

1. Sift the flour into a bowl and stir in the oats, sugar, nutmeg and cinnamon. Add the butter and mix in with a pastry blender or the prongs of a fork.

2. Place the apple slices in the base of the slow cooker and add the apple juice. Sprinkle the flour mixture evenly over them.

3. Cover and cook on low for 5½ hours. Serve hot, warm or cold, with single cream or natural yogurt.

This rich, creamy rice dessert is a really comforting treat on cold winter days. You can serve it with canned or stewed fruit if you like.

Rice Pudding

Ingredients

140 g/5 oz short-grain rice

1 litre/1¾ pints milk

115 g/4 oz sugar

1 tsp vanilla extract

To decorate

ground cinnamon

4 cinnamon sticks

 Serves 4

Preparation time: 5 minutes, plus 15–20 minutes pre-cooking

Cooking time: 2 hours

1. Rinse the rice well under cold running water and drain thoroughly. Pour the milk into a large, heavy-based saucepan, add the sugar and bring to the boil, stirring constantly. Sprinkle in the rice, stir well and simmer gently for 10–15 minutes. Transfer the mixture to a heatproof dish and cover with foil.

2. Place the dish in the slow cooker and add boiling water to come about one-third of the way up the side. Cover and cook on high for 2 hours.

3. Remove the dish from the slow cooker and discard the foil. Stir the vanilla extract into the rice, then spoon it into heatproof glasses or bowls. Dust lightly with ground cinnamon and decorate with cinnamon sticks.

This easy, yet very appealing dessert is great for dinner parties but not really suitable for serving to children.

Blushing Pears

Ingredients

6 small ripe pears

225 ml/8 fl oz ruby port

200 g/7 oz caster sugar

1 tsp finely chopped crystallized ginger

2 tbsp lemon juice

whipped cream or Greek yogurt, to serve

Serves 6

Preparation time: 15 minutes, plus cooling and chilling

Cooking time: 4 hours

---

1. Peel the pears, cut them in half lengthways and scoop out the cores. Place them in the slow cooker.

2. Mix together the port, sugar, ginger and lemon juice in a jug and pour the mixture over the pears. Cover and cook on low for 4 hours until the pears are tender.

3. Leave the pears to cool in the slow cooker, then carefully transfer to a bowl, cover and chill in the refrigerator until required.

4. To serve, partially cut each pear half into about 6 slices lengthways, leaving the fruit intact at the stalk end. Carefully lift the pear halves onto serving plates and press gently to fan out the slices. Serve with whipped cream or yogurt.

This is a sophisticated version of the popular pudding using panettone, a light-textured Italian Christmas cake flavoured with citrus rind and sultanas.

Italian Bread Pudding

Ingredients

unsalted butter, for greasing

6 slices panettone

3 tbsp Marsala wine

300 ml/10 fl oz milk

300 ml/10 fl oz single cream

100 g/3½ oz caster sugar

grated rind of ½ lemon

pinch of ground cinnamon

3 large eggs, lightly beaten

double cream, to serve

Serves 6

Preparation time: 20 minutes, plus cooling and chilling

Cooking time: 2½ hours

1. Grease a pudding basin and set aside. Place the panettone on a deep plate and sprinkle with the Marsala wine.

2. Pour the milk and cream into a saucepan and add the sugar, lemon rind and cinnamon. Gradually bring to the boil over a low heat, stirring until the sugar has dissolved. Remove the pan from the heat and leave to cool slightly, then pour the mixture onto the eggs, beating constantly.

3. Place the panettone in the prepared dish, pour in the egg mixture and cover with foil. Place in the slow cooker and add enough boiling water to come about one-third of the way up the side of the dish. Cover and cook on high for 2½ hours until set.

4. Remove the dish from the slow cooker and discard the foil. Leave to cool, then chill in the refrigerator until required. Loosen the sides of the pudding and turn out onto a serving dish. Serve with cream on the side.

Index